MY LIFE OF GRACE

"Suffering is present in everyone's life, starting from as young as we can remember up to our last days. Many often seem to be bogged down by the immense weight of suffering, but Peter Le shares the lessons and joy that can be learned through such trials. He uses many stories from his life that explain how he used his faith and wisdom to have a new perspective on what suffering can bring. This book is a great source of direction and inspiration for those seeking to become better, more well-rounded individuals who are able to tackle any problem that life may present to them."

Fr. Hy Nguyen, PSS
Rector of Assumption Seminary
San Antonio, Texas

"Chock-full of tenderness, compassion, and lessons for the path of redemptive suffering, *My Life of Grace* is a true balm for anyone facing challenging moments along life's journey. Le weaves personal vignettes with treasured Church teaching to accompany us with kindness and remind us of the hope we have in God's never-ending love and nearness. Whether you're facing hardship yourself, acting as a caregiver, or seeking to provide solace for a friend in a difficult phase of life, this book is the perfect companion."

Lisa M. Hendey
Author of *The Grace of Yes*

"Le's inspirational and powerful real-life stories of his journey as a refugee and survivor of cancer is a must-read for anyone who has ever struggled with pain, loss, illness, or doubt. It gives clarity and meaning to suffering, and it is a strong testament to the triumph of our Catholic faith in the face of unimaginable hardship. Readers, especially young people, will come to a greater understanding of God's love, even in the darkest of times."

Young Hoang
President of the National Executive Committee
Vietnamese Eucharistic Youth Movement

"We naturally fear suffering, yet there is a joy and meaning in suffering that the saints know better than anyone else. This joy comes when we learn the way of depending on God's grace. In this book, filled with wisdom gained through his own redemptive suffering, Le shares his discovery of finding joy amid his many trials and painful realities. I believe this book will be a great encouragement and inspiration to each one of us who applies its wisdom; we too will become graced men and women."

Bob Schuchts
Author of *Be Healed*

MY LIFE OF GRACE

How I Found Hope and Purpose in Suffering

Peter "Graceman" Le

AVE MARIA PRESS Notre Dame, Indiana

Scripture texts in this work are taken from the *New American Bible, revised edition* © 2010, 1991, 1986, 1970 Confraternity of Christian Doctrine, Washington, DC, and are used by permission of the copyright owner. All Rights Reserved. No part of the *New American Bible* may be reproduced in any form without permission in writing from the copyright owner.

© 2023 by Peter Le

All rights reserved. No part of this book may be used or reproduced in any manner whatsoever, except in the case of reprints in the context of reviews, without written permission from Ave Maria Press®, Inc., P.O. Box 428, Notre Dame, IN 46556, 1-800-282-1865.

Founded in 1865, Ave Maria Press is a ministry of the United States Province of Holy Cross.

www.avemariapress.com

Paperback: ISBN-13 978-1-64680-257-9

E-book: ISBN-13 978-1-64680-258-6

Cover images © Getty Images, Unsplash, and Wikimedia Commons.

Cover and text design by Andy Wagoner.

Printed and bound in the United States of America.

Library of Congress Cataloging-in-Publication Data is available.

In memory of Fr. Philip M. Tighe,
a priest from the Diocese of Raleigh
1962–2020

Contents

Introduction	xiii
Part One: Call Me "Graceman"	1
Redemptive Suffering: To Be "Sick for the Lord"	4
My Early Story	7
Coming to America	11
United with Christ in His Passion and Glory	14
Part Two: The School of Suffering	17
Why Be "Sick for the Lord"?	21
Suffering as Penance	28
The Nails of Our Cross	34
Choose Joy	38
Silence Is Golden	42
Grace in Suffering	46

The Ecstasy of God's Love	51
Song of Sorrow	55
When Temptation Comes	59
Part Three: The Gift of Suffering	63
Tears of Love	66
Act of Surrender	70
Facing Reality	73
The Way of Abandonment	77
Conversation with My Son	81
Battle Fatigue	85
When God Speaks Forgiveness	89
Suffering Is a Sign	92
Go to Our Lady of Sorrows	96
Becoming God's "Love Dumpster"	100
The Blessing of Chronic Illness	103
The Desert of Redemptive Suffering	106
Part Four: The Way to New Life	109

The End of the Road	114
A New Kind of Love	118
Patience in Dying	121
Finishing the Race	125
A Miniature of Heaven	129
Part Five: The Gift of Consolation	133
History of Our Lady of Lavang	135
Novena to Our Lady of Lavang	139
Conclusion	141
Notes	142

Introduction

I received God's consolation in my time of sickness; now, it's my season and time to write about it. The central point of this book that I want to share with you, the reader, is that to experience this consolation is to move toward redemptive suffering.

To begin, I shall let my prayer rise before God like incense and make it known that "Lord, the one you love is sick" (Jn 11:3, New International Version). This is from the Gospel of John, when Mary and Martha, the sisters of Lazarus, inform Jesus that Lazarus, whom Jesus loves, is sick. Thus, I shall imitate Mary and Martha by writing these reflections and prayers to let Jesus know of my sufferings. In doing so, I come to discover *a moment of grace*. In this intimate time I open my heart and soul, clothe myself with a humble heart and contrite spirit, and gently whisper, "Lord, it is I; the one you love is sick." In that moment, the spirit of God the Father's grace comes to my assistance, enlightens my thinking, and transforms my way of life by emptying my old wineskins and pouring new wine into fresh wineskins. These moments of grace turn a sinner like me into a man who is truly "Graceman."

As you continue to read this book, I hope you discover that the story of Graceman is yours too. I pray that you will continue to experience moments of grace as you turn and flip the pages of this book. And I pray that in each moment that you face adversity you will recognize God's grace in you as well. With the gifts of the Holy Spirit, God helps us to overcome our afflictions. I hope this story will help you to encounter God's consolation in your time of sorrow.

Part One
Call Me "Graceman"

> The greatest grace that God can give [someone] is to send him a trial he cannot bear with his own powers—and then sustain him with his grace so he may endure to the end and be saved.
>
> —*St. Justin Martyr*

This quote from St. Justin Martyr is a summary of my life. My greatest trial began in the fall of 2018. The oncologist at the University of North Carolina at Chapel Hill informed me that I had thyroid cancer and might have only six months to live. To have any hope of recovery, I needed to go through extensive surgery and countless tests and procedures.

And so, for the next four years, my body was in deep and constant pain, and all aspects of my life slowly broke down. I was living, yet I was also dying. I have traveled to five different cancer centers throughout the States for treatments, been seen by nearly three dozen oncologists, had two back-to-back surgeries, completed a month-long course of radiation and chemotherapy, and taken a mountain of medications to keep my body alive. By the grace of God, I have endured the greatest trials—and yet

Part One: Call Me "Graceman"

I am blessed, for I received God's consolation on my bed of pain. His helping hand has been my restoration from sickness to health, from mourning into dancing, and from weeping into laughter.

If you are reading this book, perhaps you understand this kind of suffering—what I like to call the "school of suffering." If you struggle to see the purpose of your suffering or struggle to see it as a source of grace, then I invite you to keep reading. I pray that God will use my experience to help you encounter his grace.

In addition to the physical toll suffering takes on the body—including both the disease and the treatment itself, which are a kind of "thorn in the flesh"—our emotions often intensify the pain. Day and night, I have been bombarded with distress, deep pain, and sorrow. I have been forced to contemplate my own mortality and wonder how my death will affect my loved ones.

And yet, even on this level, I have experienced God's consolation, mercy upon mercy, and grace upon grace. For this reason, I slowly realized that I have nothing to fear, not even death. I started to recognize the gift of grace in suffering and acknowledge the gifts and fruits of the Holy Spirit that moved me beyond my fear and toward understanding.

Despite taking a beating from this horrible thorn in my flesh, I am still living gracefully and joyfully. As for the remainder of my life, I shall ask Jesus and Our Lady for the grace that allows my wounded body to be its own source of grace for the salvation of myself and others. I am greatly blessed to have received God's consolation in

Part One: Call Me "Graceman"

my sickness. These are not just words. This is a fact and testimony to the Gospel that "he wounds, but he binds up; he strikes, but his hands give healing" (Jb 5:18). I am profoundly grateful for the gift of life and to be able to write about God's consolation so others might have hope and find that the living God is always with us, especially in a time of sickness.

At many times in the Bible when God poured his grace into an individual's life he gave them a new name: Abram became Abraham and Saul became Paul. Moving forward, I have chosen a new name to acknowledge God's hand in my life and the work of the Holy Spirit. I am Graceman, a sinner whom God loves, and I receive God's consolation in my time of sickness. I pray that my story is your story, and I hope the story of Graceman will increase your spirit of hope. I know that hope is joy and a source of grace and wisdom.

Redemptive Suffering: To Be "Sick for the Lord"

In the next section of this book I will write about the "school of suffering" and the gift of redemptive suffering. Since being diagnosed with stage four thyroid cancer, I have had a new job to serve the Lord. My job is "to be sick for the Lord."

As a Christian, I must believe that God loves me. "For God so loved the world" (Jn 3:16) that he always has ways to save the people of the world, especially in times of sickness. When I am sick, I suffer. As a person with faith, I shall always remember that sufferings come from God for my benefit. It has a purpose because "here below pure love cannot exist without suffering" (St. Bernadette). Furthermore, my pain is an invitation to unite with the Lord's Passion. The suffering Christ is on the Cross, and now my suffering shall be united with him. This is my basic understanding of the meaning of redemptive suffering, as St. John Paul II explained in his apostolic letter *Salvific Doloris* (*On Redemptive Suffering*). Redemptive suffering allows me to "be sick for the Lord" by willingly uniting my pain with the Lord's Passion. This powerful medicine can bring the healing that science fails to offer. Why?

First, through redemptive suffering my pain becomes a sacred gift for my own salvation. Suffering can also teach me humility, the greatest virtue and the key to unlocking the vault of heaven.

Second, I gain a renewed purpose in choosing to be sick for the Lord. Sickness is a painful reality that can break a person spiritually, morally, mentally, physically, and intellectually. But holding on to faith—as well as a sense of humor—helps me to embrace my sickness gracefully and joyfully. In doing so, God leads me through a new pathway to a new understanding, vision, and purpose, along with a life that is filled with grace, peace, hope, and love.

Third, the reality of life indicates that it's not always possible to avoid unloved events such as pain and suffering. Thus, when they come my way, I must learn to stay calm and have both the freedom to love these unloved situations and the courage to face them. As a sinner, I know I am weak, subject to temptations, attracted to vices, and afraid of pain and suffering. This is not a holistic way to live, and so I must learn to be brave, courageous, and to humbly embrace suffering. My suffering is not the end of the world. Thus, I must put up a fight by continuing to live my life to the fullest and not falling into dark despair. I can do this with the help of the Holy Spirit.

In short, suffering is a natural human experience. Since God is in the business of compassion, he doesn't want his creatures—created in his image—to be in pain. But because of original sin, suffering entered the world. Even so, God always gives his creatures the grace and courage to bear it. One of the ways that you and I can bear our suffering is to unite it with the suffering Christ on the Cross. It's a small living sacrifice that we can offer up for God's glory and the redemption of the body. Through it all, if we learn to suffer well in this way, our suffering is redemptive and has the power to make us more like a member of Christ's Mystical Body. Furthermore, as you continue to discover my story, you shall see that what I say about God's consolation is true. If it can happen to me, it can also happen to you, for "there is no partiality with God" (Rom 2:11–16).

As for me, I am a person living with a disability. My whole life is colored with various sufferings, including my earliest childhood memories. Add to my list that I am now living with terminal cancer. Despite these inconveniences, by the grace of God, I am Graceman, a sinner whom God loves. For that reason, though I suffer all kinds of afflictions, I am going to overcome them, just like St. Paul did (see 2 Corinthians 4:8). Please allow me to tell you some of my stories so you can see my disability as the source of my ability to live gracefully and joyfully. In the end, I hope that on the day of my departure from this life the suffering Christ shall remember me for suffering well for his sorrowful Passion and welcome me into heaven. My heart will leap up with joy and exult in the Lord on that day.

My Early Story

Soon after I was born, I was enrolled in the "school of suffering" and discovered that life is hard. Born in war-torn Vietnam, I encountered many hardships: violence, childhood sickness, years of family separation in refugee camps, living in foreign lands, and more sickness. Because of these harsh circumstances, I faced pain and suffering at an early age. Thus, I quickly learned many valuable lessons about life.

First, life is complicated, and the rules of engagement are not clearly defined. Take health, for example. Instinctively, I want a healthy, easy, uncomplicated lifestyle. But that's not always possible, and it might not be the best pathway for me, spiritually speaking. Without suffering I might become proud and arrogant. Therefore, I need to face certain afflictions, for I know God has allowed these things into my life because it builds my character.

Second, I find the school of suffering is one of the best ways to learn about life. Through real-life experiences, I quickly develop characteristics and obtain certain qualities that help me adapt to many situations. The school of suffering is a package that contains many difficult experiences and harsh lessons. The school will force me to confront reality directly. Many of these experiences and lessons are painful and extremely difficult. However, the rewards are great, and there is much wisdom in facing these adversities. These pearls of wisdom shall serve me well, especially in dealing with other kinds of pain and suffering.

As for me, the school of suffering shaped me into who I am today. It helped me build confidence in dealing with difficult situations and not be afraid of hardship. I learned how to survive and navigate through various trials and tribulations. For Christians, the school of suffering is also the school of grace. With grace and the work of the Holy Spirit, we find the strength and courage to go on with life, no matter what situation we are in. Each experience of adversity becomes a great adventure, an opportunity to receive God's grace in a new way.

Early on, I learned to place confidence in God's grace and trust that everything will be all right. Whenever life gives you lemons, as the saying goes, make lemonade. Here are some of the lemons that I encountered. By the grace of God, I learned to make much lemonade.

I was born in Vietnam during the war. During that time, Vietnam was the focal point of the Cold War between the United States and the Soviet Union. At one year old I contracted polio, which left both my legs paralyzed—the left leg being more severely affected and shorter than the right leg.

Living with polio has been a bittersweet experience. As a child with a disability, I depended on crutches and braces to walk. I quickly learned to accept it as part of life. My disability taught me to adapt to many circumstances and

NEW

A new Book from
Fr. Peter John Cameron, O.P.

A Brief Primer on *Prayer*

MAGNIFICAT / Aleteia

40 short essays to nourish your meditation during Lent

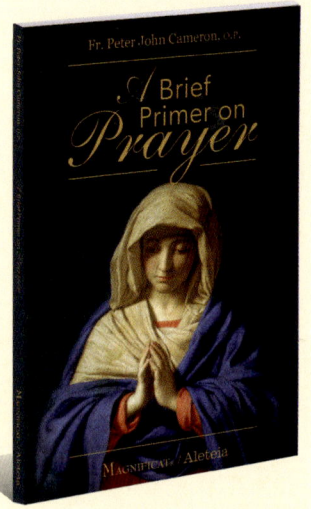

A Brief Primer on Prayer
By Fr. Peter John Cameron, O.P.

Explore the riches and benefits of prayer

US $9.95*

*Special price: 23% off the retail price of $12.95 for MAGNIFICAT subscribers

Softcover
120 pages • 5 x 7.75 in.
Also available as an eBook

Father Cameron is the Founding Editor-in-Chief of MAGNIFICAT. He is now Editor-in-Chief of the Catholic website Aleteia.org.

A thoughtful and loving

My Early Story

find ways to overcome them. Living with a disability, I am bombarded with challenges and have important choices to make, such as whether I am acting "to be better" or "to be bitter." While facing these challenges has not been easy, I improved as I grew up dealing with these physical limitations. My disability served as a teacher, under whom I learned to be a better person. My disability is my ability to live out my life gracefully and joyfully.

Life without my parents. After the war, people fled from living under the new Communist government, which had imposed martial law throughout the country. My parents allowed me to escape and seek freedom, along with my uncle and his son. Of all the events of my life, if there was one moment that I could go back to, I would choose the moment when I said goodbye to my mother on the day of my departure. I still remember vividly that day's color, smell, and feeling.

My mom took me to a crowded and noisy bus station early in the morning. As I got on the bus, I sat by the window and looked out to see my mother. As the bus started moving, I saw a teardrop on my mother's face. Never in my life did I see her tears, except on that day.

As an innocent child with a disability, I didn't understand how that experience would shape me into the man I am today. But if I could, I would paint an image of that moment, the last moment of my childhood. For the next fourteen years, I grew up without my parents and became "a man without a country," for I could not return to Vietnam. This experience robbed me of my childhood.

Losing my homeland. Those who joined the mass exodus in the early 1980s came to be known as the "boat people." I was one of the millions of boat people. The journey toward freedom in a tiny wooden boat, packed with about fifty other people, took five or six days on the open water of the Pacific Ocean. My boat was rescued by an American oil tanker ship, which dropped us off in Thailand. After a year of living in Thailand at two different refugee camps, my uncle applied for a visa to live in America. We were accepted, but first, we needed to transfer to the Philippines to learn about America. So, I settled in my third refugee camp in the Philippines. After sixteen months I came to live in Houston, Texas, when I was thirteen years old.

Coming to America

I missed my parents dreadfully—and yet, God did not forsake me during those years. Growing up in America, I had many great role models. Though my parents were in Vietnam, God sent many good and holy people who looked out for and cared for me. Along with that, I experienced many blessings. Eventually, I went to college, graduated with a degree in computer engineering, and worked as a computer programmer. Shortly after that, all my immediate family came to America from Vietnam under the Orderly Departure Program, sponsored by the American government. At last, we were together again as a family after fourteen years of separation. As they started a new life with me, I became like a parent to them because I had to care for them and show them what it was like to live in America.

After several months of working and reuniting with my parents, I joined the Dominicans (Order of Preachers) in 1995, hoping to become a priest one day. In the four years that followed, I was constantly pulled between my love for God and my longing for family.

Ultimately, through my discernment, I left religious life in 1999. I moved to Boston and worked at Harvard Medical School. After work, I took graduate courses at Harvard University as part of the perks of my job. Two years later, I was involved in one of America's most prominent human trafficking cases, where I served a subpoena as a federal witness. Shortly after, I met my future wife, a medical doctor; I moved to North Carolina when she moved there. Three years later, I married her. Together, we have had two lovely children.

In 2014, my wife and I formed a nonprofit medical clinic, St. Joseph Primary Care, to serve the poor and our neighbors. Then, in 2018, I discovered that I had metastatic (follicular) thyroid cancer. Although I lived in North Carolina, I went to MD Anderson Cancer Center in Houston for my treatments, including monthlong radiation treatment and two surgeries. Today, I am on lifelong chemotherapy at Duke Cancer Institute in North Carolina.

I have spent the past four years battling cancer, and by the most amazing grace of God I am still alive and able to write about the experience. As I write this page, my cancer is still inside me, and I am still getting chemotherapy treatment. Looking back, those four years were truly years of grace. Despite many sleepless nights dealing with pain, loneliness, hopelessness, confusion, and distress, I was enlightened by grace and filled with joy, excitement, hope, and awe. Thus, I am glad and rejoice in what has happened to me. I received God's consolation in my time of sickness. This is my greatest joy because it overshadowed all my anguish.

Receiving God's consolation is like holding on to a cup of blessings that includes God's grace, love, mercy, power, wisdom, endurance, and courage. I now taste and drink this cup of blessings and find that what once seemed impossible is possible. I hope that you will find the courage to face your hardships as you continue to read the rest of this book.

I hope the story of Graceman will empower you to see that everything is grace and will keep you from falling into sadness or despair. And if you do find yourself distressed and hopeless, that's all right too. But I hope you don't linger there for too long. Like me, I hope you can turn your sorrow into prayer by allowing your pain to be united with the suffering Christ. Soon, I hope God's consolation comes to you as it did for me. God is faithful and unchanging. It happened to me, and it will happen to you as well.

I pray and hope that you take courage in suffering and ask God for the strength to bear your pain gracefully. Ask God for help and be patient in your asking. As St. Padre Pio reminded us, "Pray, hope, and don't worry."

Among the richest gifts I have received in the school of suffering is a rediscovery of the rich devotional traditions of the Catholic Church. These devotions reminded me—as I hope they will remind you—that none of us suffers alone. Whatever you are enduring, you can ask for help: the Father's grace, the love of the suffering Christ, the gift of the Holy Spirit, the consolation of our Blessed Mother Mary, and the intercession of the whole community of angels and saints. You can also be strengthened by the sacraments of the Church and the prayerful support of family, friends, doctors, and nurses. You are not alone on this battlefield. Do not be afraid, and take the courage to enter the school of suffering. Living and thinking this way will help you to make the greatest evil in your life your greatest happiness, as it did for me.

United with Christ in His Passion and Glory

Sickness has followed me throughout my life. It was through this pain that I discovered God's saving grace in redemptive suffering: I learned to unite my sufferings with the Passion of Jesus Christ so that one day I might share in his glory. This is the purpose of all suffering: to draw us closer to Jesus, our strength, our hope—and to his mother, who always consoles her children in their suffering—whether that suffering consists of physical, emotional, spiritual, or mental pain.

How are you suffering today? Whatever it is you are experiencing right now, I pray that this book will shine a light of hope for you, that my own suffering will not be in vain but will continue to bear fruit. I want to spend the rest of my life affirming God's grace and mercy and testifying to the hope and peace I have found by uniting my own sufferings with the Passion of Christ.

The Blessed Mother is intimately connected to this experience as well. In part five of this book, you will find an exercise to help you pray for healing for yourself or your loved ones. This prayer is dedicated to Our Lady of Lavang, the Mother of Vietnam, who for more than two hundred years has comforted suffering Christians in

United with Christ in His Passion and Glory 15

times of persecution. She is a powerful intercessor for you right now, wherever you are in your "journey of hope."

Additionally, when you pray to Our Lady through the prayers that I wrote in parts two, three, and four, please note that I tried to imitate the prayers of St. Alphonsus Liguori in his *Preparation for Death: Considerations on Eternal Truths*.

Remember that nothing in the human experience is without purpose if we offer it back to God. I hope that the Father's grace, the suffering Christ, and the Holy Spirit—who inspires me to write and to experience God's consolation in times of sickness—are also in you. My God, the God of all consolations, is your God and your consolation. What inspires me will inspire you. My source of grace is yours as well. Let's begin to unfold the story of Graceman by presenting "Lord, the one you love is sick."

Part Two
The School of Suffering

> Enter through the narrow gate; for the gate is wide and the road broad that leads to destruction, and those who enter through it are many. How narrow the gate and constricted the road that leads to life. And those who find it are few.
>
> —*Matthew 7:13–14*

The school of suffering is a form of the narrow gate. What is the school of suffering? Let me begin by painting an image for you.

One day, I was sick to the point of nearly dying, in such great pain that I could hardly move. Desperate for some relief, I turned my thoughts to the spirit of God and asked him to visit me.

At that moment, it was as if the gate of heaven opened wide: the suffering Christ, along with his mother, came to visit me on my bed of pain. With the help of the Holy Spirit, I received great wisdom from this holy engagement. Jesus gently invited me to take courage, pick up my cross, and follow him to Golgotha. Then Our Lady put on her mantle as Our Lady of Lavang and spoke to me in my native tongue, Vietnamese, saying, "Do whatever he tells you" (Jn 2:5). Out of obedience I joined them, and we began to take a road trip to Calvary together.

That is the image of the school of suffering. Jesus and his mother are always very near to those who suffer, to help us bear what we must, so that one day we too will be ready for heaven. God permits this suffering by his grace, because in this school we learn to let go of what does not matter in this life and to grow in the virtues we will need in the next.

Sickness is a great teacher of humility, and the school of suffering is a school of grace. Thus, there are countless gifts of wisdom that I can learn from this school. I hope that when you finish this book you shall see suffering not as something evil but as an inevitable reality in this fallen world that God ultimately uses for our benefit.

One of the first things I learned in the school of suffering was that when we offer our sufferings to God, he allows us to unite ourselves with the redemptive work of Christ in remarkable ways.

In November 2018, I was sent for a biopsy of the tumor on my back, which was the size of a lemon. After navigating a mountain of medical records, my wife and I went to the MD Anderson Cancer Center in Texas. It was a thousand miles away from our home in North Carolina, and after the first day there my wife had to go back to care for our two young children. So, I was completely alone at the cancer center in excruciating pain.

My biopsy was scheduled for two o'clock in the afternoon. Upon entering the room, the staff gave me a gown and asked me to take off my shirt. I felt like I was being

Part Two: The School of Suffering

stripped naked. Then a doctor came into the room and explained that she needed to use a long needle to puncture my skin in order to reach the tumor. To do that, she would use a small medical hammer, and I would hear multiple "pounding sounds." The needle would be pushed deep into my skin until it reached the tumor, and she would take out a small tissue sample.

Without fully comprehending the pain I was about to receive, I lay facedown on a small table, stretched out my hands, and got ready. The doctor slowly pulled down my gown to see the tumor on my back. As I closed my eyes, ready for the procedure, I thought I knew vaguely what to expect. But I didn't realize the intensity of the pain that would be inflicted on my fragile body. *Pow*—the first pounding sound from the small hammer hitting the long needle deep into my skin. Another *pow* sound, and then more and more pounding sounds. Each blow was excruciatingly painful. I bit my tongue, squeezed my hands tightly, and endured the long agony. To cope with the pain, I placed myself at the foot of the Cross. There, I visualized the nails that went into the hands and feet of Jesus. I closed my eyes and thought of Jesus crucified on the Cross.

Slowly, the long needle penetrated deep into my skin and finally reached the tumor.

Oh! My Lord and my God!

It was the most painful experience that I have encountered. I was not just in pain from the cancer now, but also from the long needle that directly hit my tumor. It was the worst pain imaginable, and I lack words to describe it. I didn't know how I made it out of that procedure. Maybe I made it because instead of focusing on the pain, I took each pounding sound and placed myself standing in front of the Cross, watching each nail go into the Body of Jesus. This experience helped me to take my mind away from my pain.

In the agony of my suffering, I learned to turn my pain into prayers. With each needle, I silently called out, "Lord." I called eight times before it ended. Was it I who was strong? Or was it God's power in Jesus working in me? I wanted to think so, for I knew I was weak. If it weren't for God's power and grace, I would not have been able to endure the most agonizing experience of my adult life. Shortly after, the medical oncologist had a name for my illness: stage four of metastatic (follicular) thyroid cancer.

Once I understood the full extent of my disease, the cancer treatment began, and I clung to the mercy of God. My journey had a rough start. There were a lot of hopeful moments after the surgery. But soon, I was slammed with disappointing results.

I quickly discovered the meaning of the phrase "battle suffering." I learned how to win the battle: I must fight. The first step is not falling into despair and staying calm. This is where the school of suffering can begin; this is how I learned what suffering is and how to find the strength, courage, and wisdom to bear it. And the same can be true, my friend, for you, as you continue to study in this school along with me.

Why Be "Sick for the Lord"?

> Sacrifice and offering you did not desire, but a
> body you prepared for me.... Behold, I come
> to do your will, O God.
>
> —*Hebrews 10:5, 7*

In the school of suffering, there is really only one important task. It is "to be sick for the Lord." This assignment is a statement of obedience, a declaration of my intention to enter the school of suffering and to be enlightened by the nature of pain.

This doesn't mean that I ought to ignore or abandon medical treatment! It would be foolish to dismiss the medical professional community; I depend on their expertise to alleviate as much of my bodily pain as possible. Nevertheless, as a person with faith, I need to integrate my spirituality as part of a comprehensive treatment plan.

Having said that, suffering is often a big cross that God asks me to carry. I intend to accept this cross as an invitation to follow Jesus and to try to be faithful to the Gospel as Jesus commanded me. "Whoever does not carry his own cross and come after me cannot be my disciple" (Lk 14:27). I want to follow Jesus, and my sickness is a good opportunity to live out my faith. Thus, I hope that you, too, can pick up your cross in the midst of your pain and suffering and follow Jesus.

In my time of sickness, I recognize that the transition from health to sickness can be a new season. It's a moment of grace when I can rapidly pray, act, work, love, and not despair. "Being sick for the Lord" is a form of humility in which I embrace limitations. With this acceptance, I shall come to see that the love of God is waiting to enfold me. With the help of Jesus and his mother, Our Lady, I shall carry my cross calmly and peacefully. I shall adopt these words of wisdom from St. Francis de Sales: "Do as much as you can as well as you can. Strive to see God in all things without exception, and consent to his will joyously. Do everything for God, uniting yourself to him in word and deed. Walk very simply with the Cross of the Lord and be at peace with yourself."[1] If I bear my cross courageously, as St. John Vianney teaches, it will carry me to heaven.

Moreover, this school of suffering is a great teacher and contains many pearls of wisdom. In suffering, I come to see God's grace, peace, hope, love, and learn to celebrate the gift of life. With God's grace, I hope to share my journey with you in order that you might also discover how to deal with pain and suffering patiently and peacefully. Thus, my journey is also your journey. Whatever trial and tribulation that you are facing, I pray that you humbly come to God and ask him for the grace to bear it. In my experience, I know that when we come to God with a humble spirit he will give us abundant strength. This is how our suffering loses its sting and its bitterness.

Why Be "Sick for the Lord"? 23

Are you now being invited to experience a new season of suffering? As you enter this school, allow yourself to "be sick for the Lord," accepting your new reality of being sick and rejoicing in the gift of suffering. Ask God and Our Lady for the grace to unite your pain and suffering with the suffering Christ, which shall be your greatest reward.

In addition, our God is full of compassion. He gives us strength to bear our hardship via grace and the gifts of the Holy Spirit. He knows what he is doing and will not give us crosses that we cannot bear. Furthermore, the gift of faith allows us to see that where there is pain and suffering, God's grace is there to help us. Where there is sorrow, God's consolation is there to comfort us. So, take courage for knowing "Happy the one whom God reproves! The Almighty's discipline do not reject. For he wounds, but he binds up; he strikes, but his hands give healing" (Jb 5:17–18).

How long will we be in this school? Our time is in God's hands. When I was first diagnosed with cancer the oncologist told me that I had six months to live; it has now been more than four years since my diagnosis. And now, after living with polio for more than fifty years, I am also dealing with polio-related health issues. Whatever happens to me, I shall remain faithful by carrying my cross and following Jesus. That is my Christian mentality, and I pray for God the Father's grace to grant me the strength to bear my cross faithfully.

I believe the Lord still has a plan for my life, even as I suffer. I tell my family and friends that I don't have cancer or polio; I only have crosses to bear. This is not a denial. But it's a statement that the greatest evils in my life have become my greatest happiness.

In this school of suffering, there are four things I've found to be true about "being sick for the Lord."

First, suffering is unavoidable, something no one can escape. After all, to be human is to be sick.

Second, suffering is a gift—it is not evil, but something God intends for my benefit.

Third, suffering has meaning. People without faith may be bitter when they suffer, but people with faith can experience redemptive suffering and the powerful healing that medicine and science fail to offer.

Finally, "to be sick for the Lord" is about spiritual growth, about bringing my pain and suffering into union with the suffering Christ. This is one of the greatest gifts of suffering.

To succeed in this journey, I learn to turn my thoughts to God, to ask him for help along with the intercession of the saints, and to participate in the life of the Church through her sacraments, devotions, and prayers. In all, I do this in the spirit of humility by acknowledging that I am a sinner, weak, and that I can do nothing without God's grace. With a humble and contrite heart, I turn my thoughts to God and let the spirit of God come into my heart. On my bed of pain, the spirit of the suffering Christ rests upon my weary soul. Wherever there is Christ, the spirit of wisdom and understanding, love and mercy, counsel and strength, knowledge and holy desire are there with him. In union with the suffering Christ, I, too, shall receive these gifts of God.

In the school of suffering I am sick, poor, and needy. Thus, the spirit of God stirs my memory so that I may remember a thing or two from the past or present. Faith illuminates my intellect. Together, they serve as an agent to inspire me and enlarge my sense of hope. With hope, I am led to peace, grace, and empowered to endure and persevere. These examples are what I call being "enlightened by grace." Soon, I have the courage to face my pain and still be at peace.

This is also the time to put on the armor of faith and join the suffering Christ on the way to Calvary. With that, the gift of grace is at hand within me. I can stay calm and remain peaceful because the suffering Christ is with me. Furthermore, staying calm in a time of distress is an act of courage. It is this act that helps me to endure my trials and tribulations.

In short, "to be sick for the Lord" is a test of faith. It's here, in this place, that the sinner cries out loud to the suffering Christ and waits for the redemption of the body. It is here, on the bed of sickness, that the suffering Christ comes to meet sinners like me and does the work of the Divine Physician. When this moment of grace takes place, everything changes. Mourning turns into laughter; darkness into light; ordinary becomes extraordinary; impossible is now possible. Sinners shall recall God's works and realize the words of St. Paul to the Corinthians are true: "We are afflicted in every way, but not constrained; perplexed, but not driven to despair" (2 Cor 4:8).

Prayer

Almighty and everlasting God,
behold I come to the Sacrament of your
only begotten Son, Our Lord Jesus Christ.
I come as one infirm to the physician of life,
as one unclean to the fountain of mercy,
as one blind to the light of everlasting brightness,
as one poor and needy to the Lord of heaven and earth.
Therefore I implore the abundance of Thy measureless bounty . . .
heal my infirmity,
wash my uncleanness,
enlighten my blindness,
enrich my poverty and clothe my nakedness,
that I may receive the Bread of Angels,
the King of kings, the Lord of lords,
with such reverence and humility,
with such sorrow and devotion,
with such purity and faith,
with such purpose and intention
as may be profitable to my soul's salvation. . . .
O most loving Father, give me grace to behold forever
Thy beloved Son with His face at last unveiled,
Whom I now purpose to receive under the sacramental veil here below.
Amen.[2]

A Moment of Grace

This is a time for us to contemplate the truth, particularly the meaning of suffering. Perhaps the notion "to be sick for the Lord" is too difficult for you to accept.

I invite you to continue to read and ask yourself this question: What cross do you find most difficult to carry right now? Ask Jesus for strength and to be united with him and to gracefully carry the cross for the sake of his sorrowful Passion.

Suffering as Penance

Penance, Penance, Penance!
—*Words of the Angel at Fatima, 1917*

One thing I have yet to mention is penance. My suffering is an opportunity for penance, a turning back to God. Penance is an act of love for God and neighbor. This "pure love" is the highest call of the Christian life. Carrying my cross without complaining is the best penance I can perform. In my suffering I can unite with the suffering Christ. On my cross, I can look at Jesus Christ and confess that I am sorry for my sins and say: "Jesus, remember me" (Lk 23:42).

To be truly sorry for sin (expressed in penance) allows me to bear my cross patiently; my cross becomes lighter. On the contrary, if I start complaining, my cross becomes a burden because I am inflicting wounds that increase my suffering a hundredfold. The more I complain, the more bitter I become.

Instead of complaining, I can turn my suffering into prayer. A simple prayer like "Lord, help me" will deliver a great deal more grace than murmuring, "Why me?" Besides penance, I can also ask the Holy Spirit to help me to carry my cross. God will always help me to bear it.

Moreover, when I learn to unite my suffering with the suffering Christ and beg him to forgive my sins, I can profit greatly because Jesus says, "I have not come to call the righteous to repentance but sinners" (Lk 5:32). With that, I am a sinner, my suffering shall be my penance, and it is good for my soul. I hope one day soon, Jesus will say to me, "Today you will be with me in Paradise" (Lk 23:43).

Penance is love of God. At the beginning of my sickness, my spiritual director suggested that I go to Confession weekly and receive the sacrament of the Anointing of the Sick monthly. During this process, I learned that God created the heavens and the earth at the beginning of the Creation story. Afterward, he looked at everything he had made. He found it very good (Gn 1:31). It wasn't until Adam and Eve (the first human family) disobeyed God that sin entered the world and suffering started to spread throughout the land. As a member of the human family, the sin of disobedience to God causes me to suffer. Instead of living in paradise, I now wander in the valley of tears. Thus, I must return to God and ask for forgiveness of sin.

Moreover, St. Augustine explained that unlike the old Adam, Jesus Christ—the new Adam—obeyed the Father to the point of death and even death on the Cross. Because of his Passion, Jesus gives us—the human family—a resurrection of the dead so that our relationship with God can be restored; hence, instead of weeping in the valley of tears, I know that one day I shall go back home and live in paradise with God eternally. But for now, I need to do penance while I am taking refuge in this vale of tears.

Penance is love of neighbor. I have now come to understand why we must suffer. This question was asked to St. Bernadette Soubirous (1844–1879). She answered, "Because here below, *pure love* cannot exist without suffering."[1] I find this answer just. In her suffering, she totally united with the suffering Christ: "O Jesus, I no longer feel my cross when I think of yours."[2] Like her, I want to embrace Jesus through my suffering. It's a "devotion to Jesus, who, for the love of us, mortified his entire body on the cross."[3] Additionally, the greatest act in Jesus's life was his Passion. If Jesus had to suffer, then I, too, must suffer. These ways of thinking help me to stay calm, pick up my cross, and follow Jesus.

To help me to carry my own cross, I have learned about the life of St. Bernadette. After she had seen the Blessed Virgin Mary and the Church had acknowledged the apparition of Our Lady of Lourdes, St. Bernadette entered the convent of the Sisters of Notre Dame of Nevers. As a nun, she was assigned to the lowest place. When she became ill, she was placed in the corner of the infirmary. One day, the Mother Superior found her and asked, "What are you doing there?" St. Bernadette replied, "I am doing my job." "And what is your job?" the Mother Superior questioned. She answered, "To be sick."[4]

St. Bernadette understood—as all of us must come to understand—that the cross of suffering has a purpose: with this cross of mine, I must let go of myself and "cast myself on the cross where the suffering Christ finds myself entirely."[5] For as St. John Paul II noted in *Salvifici Doloris (On the Christian Meaning of Human Suffering)*, "It is in suffering, more than anything else, which clears the

Suffering as Penance

way for the grace which transforms human souls. Suffering, more than anything else, makes present in the history of humanity the powers of the Redemption" (*Salvifici Doloris*, February 11, 1984, no. 27).

So, here I am. I turned to the cross in a time of sickness, asking God for mercy and grace to fulfill my Christian duty—that is, to pick up my cross and follow Jesus. My new job is not just to be sick but "to be sick for the Lord." This is a time for me to accept the invitation to love God freely "in sickness and in health, and to love and cherish always." Through his Passion, Jesus Christ shows me the way to defeat suffering. It's the love of Christ that conquered suffering. Also, my relationship with God has been redeemed because Jesus is the "Lamb of God, who takes away the sin of the world" (Jn 1:29). It's now through the school of suffering that I come to discover the meaning of redemptive suffering.

In *Salvifici Doloris* St. John Paul II wrote that it is not only humans but suffering itself that is redeemed when "the Lord God will wipe away the tears from all faces" (Is 25:8). In this school, I also learn to honor God with all my heart, for better, for worse, in sickness and in health, until death opens the door to heaven. In addition, the school of suffering is where I can practice humility with courage and hope. This is a moment for me to embrace God's love, mercy, grace, forgiveness, and healing, even though I may die in the process. It is in dying that I am living for the glory of God. Living and dying are inseparable. Thus, I must learn to love both.

One important aspect of my new job—"to be sick for the Lord"—is faithfulness. I must learn to remain faithful to God. Being faithful is one of the fruits of the Holy Spirit (Gal 5:22). With the help of the Holy Spirit, in my time of sickness I can be strong under God's mighty providential care and face my bodily pain without giving in to despair. In addition, to be faithful is to trust. With this new job, I have a great opportunity to trust God as my Father. And like any good parent, my Father gives me everything that is good for me. I must learn to live that way.

I am simply a poor, weak, and needy child in my sickness. Since I "stand firm in the faith" (1 Cor 16:13), he will give me the grace to bear my pain, the strength to overcome adversity, and the peaceful assurance that I am going to be all right. With that, I shall live in the remembrance of grace, in prayer and action, in hope, until the final day that I rest in the arms of God.

These are some reasons why suffering serves as penance and why we must suffer.

Prayer

> Lord, I am now the richest man alive because I have time. There is a time for everything, including a time to be sick. Help me to accept this cup and drink it joyfully. Give me hope and strength to carry this cross rightly to the end. By God's mercy and grace, this cross of mine will carry me to heaven. So, help me, God.

Suffering as Penance

Mary, Our Lady and my Blessed Mother, my hope after Jesus, please bless me with the gift of time and do not let me waste my time. As for the remainder of my earthly time, please grant me your grace so I may remain faithful and never depart from the love God has for me now and forever. Amen.

A Moment of Grace

None of us knows how much time we have left; each moment is precious. What will you do with the time you have right now?

All of us want to remain healthy and to avoid sickness, and we try to do everything to accomplish that goal. However, the fact of life is that we don't always get what we want. Sometimes, the things we do not want, like sickness or cancer, show up unexpectedly. When this unwelcome event occurs, can we learn to accept this harsh reality?

Accepting does not mean giving up. Rather, it's an opportunity to grow in virtue, an invitation to imitate the Passion of Christ. In doing so, we may experience that the spirit that raised Jesus from the dead is also in us (Rom 8:11). Plus, in cheerfully accepting the invitation to join the suffering Christ on the way to Calvary, we also receive the crown of victory. After all, God loves a cheerful giver (2 Cor 9:7), and "God loves those who thank him even in suffering."[6]

The Nails of Our Cross

> To join two things together, there must be nothing between them, or there cannot be a perfect fusion. This is how God wants our soul to be, without any selfish love of ourselves or of others in between, just as God loves us without anything in between.
>
> —*St. Catherine of Siena*

Life is difficult, unpredictable, and full of surprises. Sometimes, life is good, and it is very easy to accept it and raise our voices in singing *alleluia*. There is a reason for gladness and rejoicing. Other times, life is not good. Then, there's a reason for sorrow, and it's very hard to keep singing because tears of sadness are getting in the way.

So far, I have talked about accepting unwelcome surprises and remaining serene in dealing with these difficult realities. But how can I remain calm during a time of chaos when pain and suffering terrorize my body?

The best way to stay calm is to turn my thoughts toward the suffering Christ and allow the Holy Spirit to move me. There are three important aspects to this statement. First, to move me toward God, I "turn my thoughts" to him and talk to him, like I talk to my friends and family. Talking

The Nails of Our Cross

to God is a form of prayer. Second, to move toward God is to surrender to the will of God. In other words, I allow my experience to unite with Jesus and his Passion. Third, in doing so, I am changing, transfiguring into something new and better. I am changing my thinking so that I can act with the will of the Holy Spirit.

To demonstrate what I mean by turning my thoughts to the suffering Christ, I use the image of "the nails of our cross." The nailing of our cross is a dreadful event that each person must face in their lifetime. No one can escape from this reality, and it causes the heart, mind, and spirit to tremble when it happens. It's a roaring moment that echoes with fear, anguish, and anxiety, and mingles with pain, suffering, confusion, and frustration. People living with cancer must face many situations like these. Pain is the nail of the cross that pierces deep into the body and soul of the person.

I learned to stay calm and not rush to judgment in these hard situations. It's a simple act, but it's an act of grace. Also, when the nail of my cross comes my way, by remaining calm I may have the courage to go to the cross, stand there, and look up to the suffering Christ. Here I am, standing at the foot of the cross, activating one of the seven gifts of the Holy Spirit, the gift of counsel. In times of trouble, I ask Jesus for strength, guidance, and wisdom to gracefully bear my cross. Trusting in God's providence, I can take these nails as a source of grace that can bind my heart and soul closer to God. When this bond occurs, I have less fear and can recognize that everything is grace. Thus, it's a gift, and it is for my benefit.

In addition, I understand that God's consolation is only given in a time of sickness. The nails of our cross that cause our minds to tremble are good because they help increase our desire to seek God. For example, when a person gets sick it's a good time to see the doctor. So, too, when there is a time of sickness and sorrow, it's a great opportunity to go to God and ask for the gift of God's consolation. To receive God's consolation is to receive God's grace, love, mercy, power, wisdom, endurance, courage, and healing. Therefore, stay calm during sickness, trial, and tribulation; we can turn our thoughts to God, asking God for help by giving us strength to bear our hardships. Be patient; be very patient in asking God. Most importantly, don't let the nails of our cross frighten us. Look at the man on the cross and not just the cross. In a time of sickness, contemplating the image of the suffering Christ can lead to great healing. It gives a sense of peace.

In due times, the Divine Physician, in his tender care, shall deliver his consolation to those who seek him. Remember that the prophet Isaiah reminded us that God's ways are not ours (see Isaiah 55:9). Thus, in asking God for help, we can only place our trust and confidence in him and have hope in God. That is all we can do. It's totally up to God to give, heal, answer our prayers, or do nothing. Sometimes, "doing nothing" is how the Lord hears our prayers. Our main job is like the prayer of St. Teresa of Avila: "Let nothing disturb you, let nothing frighten you, all things are passing away: God never changes. Patience obtains all things; whoever has God lacks nothing; God alone suffices."[1]

In short, the nailing of our cross is a time of trial. It's a way to practice faithfulness to God. If we truly believe that "whoever has God lacks nothing," let us receive the nail and see how we would react. Suffering in this way will greatly benefit us. It makes us worthy to receive God's consolation.

Prayer

My Lord, my God, and for the sake of my Jesus's sorrowful Passion, have mercy on me so that I may remain in deep union with God's will. When I am in pain, may my pain be the pain of remembrance of grace. Thank you for making me worthy of being with you, along with Our Lady, at the Cross. O my sweet Jesus, remember me.

Mary, our hope, our sweet mother, grant me the grace to stand next to you at the foot of the Cross and ponder the Mystical Body of your son, our Lord Jesus Christ.

A Moment of Grace

In what moments in your own story have you felt the nails of your cross? Can you thank Jesus for that invitation to identify with his Passion? Can you trust and believe that God can take care of your problem? If the answer is no, then ask yourself, Why? Is it because of a lack of trust and understanding? Do vices like fear, bitterness, pride, ignorance, and control get in the way? Even if the answer is yes, then *why*? Is it because you, too, have received God's consolation in your time of sickness that you say yes to the nails of your cross? Or is it something else?

Choose Joy

> If you help the person in a spirit of joy, then the help will be received joyfully, and it becomes a source of blessing to the giver and receiver.
>
> —*St. John Chrysostom*

The secret of life is to be joyful in all circumstances. So how is it possible for anyone to choose joy in times of sorrow? Maybe I ought to learn from St. Thérèse of Lisieux. Here is what she said: "When we are expecting only suffering, the least joy surprises us: Suffering itself becomes the greatest of joys when we seek it as a precious treasure."[1]

I truly find encouragement in her words. I firmly believe that suffering can be a precious treasure. Here is one such moment of "precious treasure."

Since I was first diagnosed with cancer, I have visited five cancer centers. I often travel alone because my wife must stay home to care for our two children. Being alone in this environment can be frightening and lonely. Over time, I have learned to stay focused by always turning my thoughts to Christ, particularly toward his Passion. This has allowed me to choose joy over despair.

During one of these visits to the MD Anderson Cancer Center in Houston, I was learning to maneuver around the hospital with the help of my crutches. It is a large hospital, making it harder for a person with a disability to get around. As I walked from one appointment to the next, I noticed many sad faces. Seeing their expressions, I thought of Jesus carrying his Cross toward Golgotha. I thought of how extremely lonely and painful it must have been for Jesus.

Then I saw a smile from a wife caring for her husband, a cancer patient. Her gentle smile put a smile on my own face as well. I thanked her and continued down the hall. A few more steps away from the elevator, I saw a frustrated husband trying to push his wife's wheelchair. I thanked him for helping her. He was surprised by my words and replied in a stern, loud voice, "I am trying my best." I guess he was trying to reassure himself.

After these two interactions, I thought about being a "joy giver" to these cancer patients and their caregivers—even when I was experiencing pain and suffering. One by one, I was able to distract them with a smile or a word of thanks. I started to thank the people who opened the door, the doctors, nurses, and whomever I came across.

When Jesus carried his Cross to Golgotha, there were those who did what they could to ease his pain, such as Simon of Cyrene who helped Jesus carry his Cross. There were even some women who cried for Jesus, and he said to them, "Do not weep for me; weep instead for yourselves and your children" (Lk 23:28).

I want to be like Jesus, not focusing on my pain. In doing so, I have the freedom to choose joy over sadness, laughter over tears, peace over anxiety, have hope and dreams, and not be burdened by the valley of tears that is this world.

Prayer

O Lord, I am so grateful for the gift of life. Thank you for giving me such a privilege to be alive and to be loved by you. Though my body is broken, sinful, sorrowful, and unworthy, by your grace and your wish, I shall be cleaned whiter than snow. In return, may my hands help others, feet hasten to the poor, eyes see the misery of others and tenderly care for them, ears hear the sighs and sorrows of those who weep. Lastly, may my wounded body be your source of grace for others.

O Mary! My hope after Jesus, my tender mother, please ask Jesus to wipe away all tears and sorrow on all faces here on earth. Please grant me the spirit of joy for knowing that I am a sweet child of God.

A Moment of Grace

Joy spells J (for Jesus), O (for others), and Y (for yourself). Can you find joy this way as well, by putting Jesus and others before yourself? Sometimes, the spirit of joy and happiness is the ability to see things through the lens of faith. In all things, I ought to let God increase while "I must decrease" (Jn 3:30).

These things can only be accomplished through many hours of prayer. Thus, I invite you to increase your prayer life. The Catholic Church has a vast number of ways to help the faithful to increase their prayer life, such as the Rosary, the Divine Mercy Chaplet, the Divine Office, daily Mass, meditation, novenas, Scripture, prayer books written by saints, and devotions. I hope you have a favorite way to pray and remain faithful, especially in your time of sickness. This way, peace and grace shall be with you. It's a great joy to live in this way.

Silence Is Golden

> Silence is absolutely necessary. If silence is
> lacking, then grace is lacking.
> —*St. Maximilian Kolbe*

One of the most crucial steps in this journey toward grace is developing a deep prayer life. I titled this reflection "Silence Is Golden" because it is by listening in silence that we can hear God speak and receive the treasure he wants to give us. Here, I learn to listen to the will of God. I am not doing all the talking; God does the talking.

Throughout this book, I have used the phrase "turn my thoughts to God" on numerous occasions. That is to say, I am talking to God. Now, it's time for God to talk to me. He begins talking to me by sending the Holy Spirit to open my lips, heart, and soul.

There are numerous ways for me to pray. As a Catholic person, I have discovered vast riches in the Liturgy of the Hours. But to pray to God is simply to have a dialogue with him. For example, vocal prayer is our way of talking to God while mental prayer, a form of silent prayer, is our way to listen to God and allow him to talk to us in the deepest parts of our hearts and souls. Silence is golden

Silence Is Golden

because it's a way for me to listen to the will of God. It's a meeting place between God and the sinner.

In my time of health and sickness, I often turn my thoughts to Jesus. Turning to him after daily Mass, I spend extra time with him alone, praying fervently the Liturgy of the Hours. This ritual helps me to follow St. Paul's command: "Rejoice always. Pray without ceasing. In all circumstances give thanks, for this is the will of God for you in Christ Jesus" (1 Thes 5:16–18).

Then there are other times after Mass when I close my prayer book, put away my rosary, completely shut down everything, forget my work and sickness, and cast away my anxiety and sorrow; I then stare at the cross. Sometimes, I close my eyes and put myself in the presence of the Lord. I acknowledge that I am sitting with God, and he is sitting next to me. During these moments of grace, I feel that God sends many of his angels to open my lips, heart, and soul so that I can be in deep union with him. Here is one of the prayers that I've encountered in my times of sickness and silence:

"Jesus, son of David, have pity on me!" (Mk 10:47).

O Lord, I am so tired of being sick. Have pity on me and grant me the joy of your help. Day and night, I am bombarded with trials and tribulations. I am sick, weak, and sinful. For these reasons, I find myself in a state of sorrow, lamentation, and constraint. But you, O Lord, the God of love and faithfulness, look down on my weary soul, help me crawl to the finish line, guide me to consult not with my fears of sickness but with my hopes and dreams.

Let me not be concerned about dying, but think about the gift and the wisdom of suffering and what is still possible for me to do. After all, as your child, I am still obligated to do your will and not my own. While I am at it, have pity on me, O Lord, and let my soul know and love you so that I may find joy in you; and if I fail, let me at least make progress every day, especially on my bed of pain. Let this painful moment be my song, singing *alleluia* softly. Though it sounds incomplete here on earth, one day, I shall find great joy in hope and heaven that is a complete joy.

Though I am so tired, sick, sinful, and sorrowful, bless me, O Lord, and forgive my sins. Shed upon my dark soul the brilliant light of your wisdom so that I may be enlightened and serve you with great joy. With that, by your grace, I shall discover the treasure hidden within myself ever since my baptismal grace. Grant that I may receive my request to complete my joy in this valley of tears. Blessed be the Lord, who is Three in One.[1]

Prayer

Mary, my hope and my mother, teach me to be silent so that I may learn to ponder all things. Please grant me the grace to listen well.

A Moment of Grace

How are you experiencing God's mercy in your life today? Can you be silent and be still? And at the sound of silence, can you recognize the presence

Silence Is Golden

of God within you? Now, can you sing, not just from the lips, but from your heart and soul with these words?

Christ be beside me; Christ be before me. In my time of sickness, Christ be behind me, below me, above me, on my right and left hand, all around me, in my sleep, in my sitting, in my rising, on my tongue, Christ ever be, and never to part.[2]

Grace in Suffering

> Three times I begged the Lord about this, that it might leave me, but he said to me, "My grace is sufficient for you, for power is made perfect in weakness."
>
> —*2 Corinthians 12:8–9*

In this passage from his Second Epistle to the Corinthians, St. Paul writes eloquently about the meaning of grace in suffering. This message implies that, even if I ask the Lord to take away my suffering numerous times, my requests may be rejected. The Lord sees that my suffering is for my benefit.

So, what are some of the benefits and graces that can come out of my suffering? Here are some of the most precious gifts I have received.

The gift of wisdom. To be human is to encounter pain and suffering; it is not possible to avoid it altogether. Suffering is a fact of life. Nevertheless, I am a firm believer that wherever there is pain, there is grace. This is another fact of life I ought to remember well. I know from experience that God makes up for what is lacking in me with great generosity. It's also in times of sickness that I receive

Grace in Suffering

God's consolation. Thus, it's good for me to encounter a little pain, and I accept this reality.

The gift of sanctification. When I accept pain and endure it silently, God gives me the grace to care for myself adequately. As I face whatever comes—various uncertainties, hope and despair, good and bad news—I continue to embrace my suffering. These moments of sadness become moments of grace as God continues to build me up and to purify my heart. It is in those moments that I experience the *gift* of suffering. It's a gift because the power of grace overshadows suffering. It also helps me to become a better person with a humbler spirit.

When we must endure prolonged suffering, we often must also experience a constant mix of emotions—including the fear of dying, which is constantly at the center. Sometimes these emotions are like the "angel of Satan" and exist "to beat me, to keep me from being too elated" (2 Cor 12:7). Though I dislike the experience of being beaten, I reluctantly accept it because it's good for my soul. Without suffering, I might clothe myself in pride for being so strong and healthy, or take pride in my good genes, which have kept well. Thus, I might feel that I don't need or depend on anyone, including God. But instead, I have found that to live is to suffer. There is no exception to this rule: I am humbled by the experience.

The gift of justice. As I have already said, sin is the root cause of all our suffering. And yet, suffering also provides an opportunity for penance, an expression of sorrow for sin.

Every living human is subject to sin, except Jesus the Messiah and the Immaculate Virgin Mary, full of grace, who was spared because of her Immaculate Conception.

Because I am a sinner, I must do penance for my sins. Thus, in my time of sickness and on my bed of pain, I must think of my sins and take refuge in the Sacrament of Reconciliation, where I ask God to forgive my sins. The justice of God demands that my soul must be purged and purified from sin before I can be with God. "Be holy because I [am] holy," says the Lord (1 Pt 1:16). In other words, to be with God I must be sinless.

If I don't do penance here on earth, I shall face suffering after death in purgatory. Why? Because of God's justice. It is true that God is merciful, but he is also just. In *Diary of Saint Maria Faustina Kowalska: Divine Mercy in My Soul* by St. Faustina Kowalska, God reveals to the Apostle of Mercy something about the fires of purgatory and hell: "My mercy does not want this, but justice demands it."[1]

The gift of redemption. Previously, I talked about how the school of suffering is a way to learn humility. Sometimes, there are far worse things than suffering. Pride is the best example. Having pain is good sometimes because I learn how to be humble and not get proud. I firmly believe being humble will get me to the gate of heaven and present the merits that I earned in this life. Humility will help me to get past the gate and enter heaven and see the face of God and be with him for eternity.

In addition to being humble, I have learned to be patient. Patience is an attribute of endurance, and "nothing great is ever achieved without much enduring."[2] This

Grace in Suffering

achievement goes along with perseverance, and it leads to strength, power, courage, and other virtues. Ultimately, the gift of suffering is the gift of love. God's grace is God's consolation. In suffering, God's grace illuminates and intensifies to a point beyond human reason and understanding. Therefore, grace alone is indeed sufficient (see 2 Corinthians 12:9), and it will help us to overcome any hardship.

With the gifts of wisdom, sanctification, justice, and redemption—along with some humility, patience, and holy perseverance—I can fully accept the grace in suffering.

Prayer

Ah, my God! Thank you for the gift of grace in suffering. Please teach me that my time is short here on earth so that I may gain wisdom. Sanctify me in my long-suffering, so I may endure and remain in holy perseverance in my time of sickness. Lord, please allow me to profit from the little time I have left; wait for me a little longer so I may lament my sorrow a little. I am sorry for all my sins. Pardon me and grant me the grace to love you for the future. O Mary, my hope! Please pray to Jesus for me.

A Moment of Grace

Before reading this book, what was your understanding of the meaning of "grace in suffering"? Now, I hope you have come to a new understanding of the grace in your suffering. Reflecting on your life, pay attention to moments of sadness, discouragement, and sickness. Can you see God's grace there beside the pain and suffering? Are you able to accept that as a gift? How do the gifts of wisdom, sanctification, justice, and redemption fit into your struggle? If you have a hard time putting all the pieces together, maybe you can just think about this truth: where there is pain, there is God's grace. Can you name God's grace in your struggle? I hope and pray that it is your source of strength and encouragement.

The Ecstasy of God's Love

> Prayer is an act of love. Words are not needed.
> —*St. Teresa of Avila*

God knows that humans are weak and fragile. Thus, wherever there is pain and suffering, there is also God's mercy. This mercy of God is amplified as human fragility increases.

In teaching on the levels of prayer, St. Teresa of Avila describes the highest levels of prayer, in which "the soul experiences divine reality with such intensity that it could easily fall into ecstasy. In the beginning, this sublime absorption of the faculties in God lasts but a short time . . . but as the intensity increases, it may be prolonged for several hours."[1]

I recall one time in particular, a time of raging pain, when I found myself caught up in the ecstasy of God's love. Throughout my life I have faced various trials and tribulations. And yet this one instance stands out the most, when during one of the most painful events of my life I received a rain of grace by the mercy of God. God's grace and mercy washed away my sorrow and filled me with joy, hope, peace, and satisfaction.

As I recall, a few days after a biopsy on the tumor in my back, Mr. Carcinoma was infuriated and decided to put up a fight to destroy my spirit by launching a fearful arsenal known as *pain*. On my back was a tumor the size of a lemon that terrorized my body, and the rain of pain came down hard. One night the pain awakened me at two in the morning, and for nearly four hours Mr. Carcinoma tried to knock me down by terrorizing my body with excruciating pain.

With every beat of my heart, I felt the pain like a tiny needle puncturing my heart from behind. I slowly tried to sit up and grabbed many pillows and blankets to place them on my back. I took a few medications to ease my pain, but the intense agony persisted. I stayed up all night, unable to lie down. Both my back and head poured with sweat, as though I was taking a shower.

It was during those unbearably painful moments that I experienced the ecstasy of God's love. There on my bed of nonstop, excruciating pain, the Holy Spirit lifted my dying body, mind, and spirit to the consciousness of God's presence.

I closed my eyes and placed my head down, and an image of a dead forest appeared. I saw myself on my knees, fully naked with my head down on the ground, arms outstretched, surrounded by a dead forest with no sound or color except the shade of gray. Everything surrounding me was gray, including the sky, the trees with no leaves, dead logs, and me. I saw a long log on the ground, just a few feet in front of me. As I knelt there—at each sound of

The Ecstasy of God's Love

my heartbeat—pain and more pain penetrated my heart and soul. Each heartbeat was agonizing pain.

With each beating of my heart, I cried out internally and in silence, *"Mercy."* Throughout the night, I recited this word repeatedly: *mercy, mercy, more mercy.* At six o'clock in the morning, my wife came into my room to check on me, and she saw what had happened. When she saw how much I was sweating, she went downstairs to get me a sizeable cup of cold water. I drank it all.

Two hours later, my pain had dissipated. I was feeling normal again. That night, I experienced for the very first time that I could have died due to pain. But I did not die. In that ecstasy, I discovered that I would have died but by the grace of God. I was saved by God's mercy. To save me from dying, God sent his angel to open my lips, heart, mind, and soul so that I could speak, appropriately, one last word. At the hour of my near-death experience, the one and only word that I could justify speaking rightly and justly was *mercy*. But how could I, a sinner about to go into the grave, call out to God for mercy? It must have been the angel of the Lord who came to my rescue and allowed me, one last time, to ask for God's mercy. I asked for mercy, and I received mercy. What a night and what a moment. It was not possible for me to be hallucinating and have had such an ecstasy like that.

It must have been God's mercy that allowed me to experience that most profoundly deep union with him.

Prayer

> Kyrie, Eleison / Lord, Have Mercy
> Lord, have mercy.
> Christ, have mercy.
> Lord, have mercy.

A Moment of Grace

What is your understanding of God's mercy? Contemplate (or think about) the mystery of God's mercy. When you think of God, the spirit of wisdom comes and teaches you at the level of where you are.

Is there a time in your life that was just so difficult for you to handle? How did you approach God at that time? How are you approaching him now? Is it with a humble heart and contrite spirit? Or is it like a demand for God to do this and do that?

Song of Sorrow

> In suffering, God gives strength and the soul
> practices and acquires virtue, and become
> pure, wiser, and more cautious.
>
> —*St. John of the Cross*

The day after Christmas in 2018, I found myself a thousand miles from my home in North Carolina at the MD Anderson Cancer Center in Houston, facing a thyroidectomy. It was my second surgery in six weeks. Instead of feeling sad, I turned my sorrow into a song of praise that went like this:

> I am feeling a little tired. My voice is low.
> Despite all the things that happened to my
>   body,
> it's great to be alive. I am truly blessed.
> Thank God for all the people who helped
>   and prayed for me, both near and far. Oh!
>   What a feeling.
> With this feeling, I am standing tall,
> and my head is looking up to the sky,
> showing off my wounded body for God to see,
> and letting God shower me with his grace.
> Though it hurts to look up, it's a good hurt.

> Though my voice is low, I am singing high notes
> because I am still alive.
> To be alive with grace is heaven on earth. I am content.
> Now, I shall learn to adapt to this new body of mine,
> a body that is filled with scars, pain, and suffering,
> but it feels good. I am alive.
> Christ suffered.
> As part of the Body of Christ, I must suffer too. Turning my pain and suffering
> into an acceptable gift I can carry with me,
> all the days of my life.
> These are the mysteries of life.
> I don't need to understand.
> I only need to believe, trust, and continue to have faith.
> My suffering is a gift.

These were my words, although it was somewhat unusual for the words to pour out of me as they did. In all honesty, I felt it was the spirit of God who entered into my heart and inspired me to think, write, and sing. On my own, I was not capable of turning my sorrow into a song of praise, but this was God's way to console my wounded body. He turned my sorrow into a song of gratefulness. Gratitude is a remedy to cure sorrow. If it wasn't for my suffering, I would not have been able to share all of this with you.

Song of Sorrow

Up until this point, I hope you have found my experience inspiring, and that you, too, will find God's consolation in your time of sickness. In many ways, turning my sorrow into a song of praise caused my suffering to lose its sting and bitterness. This process, in itself, is part of God's consolation. Now that I have less fear than before, I can face my suffering gracefully.

In battling with cancer, I must deal with long-suffering where everything is uncertain, and I am perfectly content with that reality. It's a small price to pay for the gift of life. However, with all the uncertainty thrown at me, I learned to remain faithful to God. This is very hard to do. It is easier to fall into sadness and despair. Now, God knows that it's not easy for me to remain faithful, so God helps me to acquire virtue and wisdom, just like what St. John of the Cross described previously. Again, all these insights are part of God's consolation in my time of sickness, and it's a great blessing to experience such wonderful grace.

Prayer

Dear God, through your Son, Jesus, you have shown me that even the most terrible suffering can be beautiful if it is your will, and if I endure it with patience and obedience. Because of Jesus, I have learned to find joy in my own suffering.

A Moment of Grace

What are some of the ways you have suffered? Are you willing to offer these troubles to the Lord and expect nothing in return? Sometimes, this is how the Lord turns our "mourning into dancing" (Ps 30:12). To expect nothing is a way to empty ourselves so that God can fill up our empty cup with his blessings.

When Temptation Comes

> God is faithful and will not let you be tried
> beyond your strength; but with the trial, he
> will also provide a way out, so that you may
> be able to bear it.
>
> —*1 Corinthians 10:13*

When the season of sickness arrives and our bodies get weak, we become vulnerable to certain kinds of temptation. And yet, we can take courage by asking God for help.

In January 2019, I went back to Houston for one last treatment. I was hopeful that the treatment would work and that I would soon be free from cancer. This time, I received a special grace: instead of staying in a hotel like on my previous trips, God led me to the perfect place for me to rest. I would be staying at the St. Catherine Convent, home of the Vietnamese Dominican Sisters.

When I arrived at the convent, a sister gave me two keys. One was the key to my room, and the other was the key to the chapel. After many days of testing and procedures, the oncologists informed me that the treatment had been unsuccessful. My cancer was now terminal. There was nothing more they could do.

I was devastated by the news. I returned to the convent heartbroken. Standing at the front door, I looked at the keys in my hand. The first was the key to my car, where I had access to the world. The world beckoned me to distraction, promising me that it could take away my sorrow by drinking like there was no tomorrow. Or I could use the second key and go to my room or open the door to the chapel.

At that moment, I felt real temptation to give in to the pull of the world, to go out and get drunk. It was late, and the winter night was cold. I was alone, lonely, sorrowful, confused, and exhausted.

The alternative, going alone to the chapel at a time like this, with bad news fresh on my mind, didn't seem like a wise choice. Going there, *alone*, in silence on a cold, shivering, and dark night to face my fear, anxiety, frustration, and great disappointment would be like facing death. Sure, the chapel was God's dwelling place. I should not have been afraid. But I was scared and had no desire to go in there.

Not knowing what to do, I stood outside for some time, trembling and weeping. I was deeply tempted to go out and get drunk, to forget the storm of emotions that had overwhelmed me. But I did not. Gracefully, I walked away from my car and entered the chapel with tears on my face.

The chapel was dark, cold, and completely silent. Holding on, I wearily sat down in one of the corner pews. I was shaking, alone in the dark with no one around but me and God. I started to cry and cry. My eyes were so full

When Temptation Comes

of tears that they coursed down my cheeks, and I caught them with my tongue. Teardrop after teardrop, I tasted them all. Every so often, I used my own tears to wash my sorrowful face.

As the commotion in my mind began to dissipate, a voice whispered gently into my ears, *"I know."* In a split second, I knew it was not just any voice. It was the voice of God's consolation: *"I know* your pain and sorrow. *I know* your disappointment. *I know* everything you're going through. *I know."*

That night, God's consolation came to me in those two simple words—"I know" contained everything I needed. That night, I discovered that where there is sorrow, there is also God's consolation. This consolation is part of God's love and mercy.

He had delivered me from temptation. And by giving me the courage to walk away from the temptation, he opened the door so my heart and soul could hear his voice. I was traumatized and didn't know what to do or say. But in the silence of the lonely night, heaven opened a door here on earth so that I could receive God's consolation in two simple words that contained every blessing. And my heart was full of joy.

Prayer

Lord, my dear Father, I kneel before you this day and praise you fervently for my present sufferings, and I give thanks for the measureless sufferings of the past. I now realize that all these sufferings are part of your paternal love, in which you chastise and purify me. And through that discipline, I now look at you without shame and terror, because I know that you are preparing me for your eternal kingdom.[1]

A Moment of Grace

Life is hard and difficult. Sometimes, it can be easy to fall into temptation as we cope with the difficulties in our lives. But this momentary relief is nothing compared to the consolation of the Lord.

Overcoming temptation is challenging. However, when God allows certain temptations to enter our life, he gives us abundant strength to bear them and ways to overcome them, if we only ask him. When we are in the state of grace, we can derive immense merit from every temptation. It helps us to live virtuously.

What temptation is facing you right now? Ask God for the grace to stay close to him, to receive his consoling presence.

Part Three
The Gift of Suffering

> If one can suffer and continue to love, one can do almost everything, even things which seem impossible.
>
> —*Catherine Doherty, Foundress of the Madonna House Apostolate*

One of the greatest gifts I have received from my illness is a deepening of the gifts of the Holy Spirit (wisdom, understanding, counsel, fortitude, knowledge, piety, and fear of the Lord), and this has led me to an understanding of redemptive suffering. While our redemption comes through Christ's sacrifice on the Cross, we participate in that sacrifice through our own suffering. Thus, our redemption is directly related to Christ's suffering, and our suffering is also linked back to our redemption.

Four years ago, when I was first diagnosed with cancer, a friend introduced me to *Salvifici Doloris*, St. John Paul II's apostolic letter from 1984. I read it and was delighted because it helped me to suffer well. In particular, it helped me to see that the temporal sufferings of this world—particularly those endured by Christ on the Cross—were to protect us from the greatest kind of suffering: the loss of eternal life. St. John Paul II writes:

> Man "perishes" when he loses "eternal life." The opposite of salvation is not, therefore, only temporal suffering, any kind of suffering, but the definitive suffering: the loss of eternal life, being rejected by God, damnation. The only-begotten Son was given to humanity primarily to protect man against this definitive evil and against *definitive suffering*. In his salvific mission, the Son must therefore strike evil right at its transcendental roots from which it develops in human history. These transcendental roots of evil are grounded in sin and death: for they are at the basis of the loss of eternal life. The mission of the only-begotten Son consists in *conquering sin and death*. He conquers sin by his obedience unto death, and he overcomes death by his Resurrection. (John Paul II, *Salvifici Doloris*, February 11, 1984, no. 14)

All my sufferings, then—from the time I contracted polio in a war zone when I was just a year old to my present battle with cancer—are not without purpose. They are part of God's plan that leads to heaven.

Early in my life, I learned two important lessons: First, I must depend on others to survive. And second, I cannot always depend on getting what I need from others; I need something better. By understanding God's purpose for our suffering, we come to understand a third important lesson: God can be trusted to give us what we need—even when the temporal suffering does not go away. He never leaves us alone in our suffering.

Part Three: The Gift of Suffering

I became a loner at a very early age, and loneliness has followed me. Because of these difficult real-life experiences, my Catholic faith emerged as my way of life, a reliable source and saving grace. My faith has become the cornerstone of my life and illuminates my intellect. Through faith, whenever I feel lonely, sick, sad, desperate, and in trouble, I can easily turn my thoughts to God.

I talk to God and seek help from him and Our Lady. And from these prayers, I always receive great strength and the ability to carry my cross. I am grateful knowing God is there to help me. Despite my hardships, there are countless moments of deep joy, satisfaction, and accomplishment. Through faith, I know these blessings are from God. In all, I learn to live in harmony with God's will in good times and in bad times.

To be harmonious is to unite. And so, redemptive suffering in a nutshell is that harmony between my suffering and the suffering of Christ. This harmony is a redemptive quality and is powered by the love of God for humanity. Because of this redemption, though I walk in the valley of tears, I fear no evil because God is with me. One day, when I receive perfect harmony, I will be with God, and God will be with me, totally. I now share with you many gifts of suffering that I have received as part of God's consolation.

Tears of Love

If I have all faith as to move mountains but do not have love, I am nothing.

—*1 Corinthians 13:2–3*

One gift of suffering is compassion, the ability to show love in spite of suffering. Without love, my suffering is in vain, and I am nothing but a loud, "resounding gong or a clashing cymbal" (1 Cor 13:1), a whiner.

With love and in my suffering, I come to unite with the suffering Christ and am able to fall in love with him. I shall merit the greatest reward—my tears of love are precious gems in the crown of victory I shall receive in heaven.

I received this gift of tears in a special way during a monthlong radiation treatment in Houston, Texas—a thousand miles away from home in North Carolina. I did a lot of writing and reflecting while I was living there in a convent. Inspired by the prayer of peace by St. Francis of Assisi, I composed my own prayer of grace:

> Lord, make my wounded body an instrument of your grace.

Tears of Love

> Where there's pain, may my soul see your grace.
> Where there's sorrow, may my spirit feel your consolation.
> Where there's sadness, may my body touch your healing sensation.
> Where there's trial and tribulation, may my will surrender to your will.
> Where there's doubt, may my conscience build trust in you.
> For where there's grace, there's peace, wisdom, and strength.
> O God, the Divine Doctor of my soul, the source of all grace, in you, and through your grace, my soul finds rest, peace, and joy.
> Lord, may I live to glorify you.
> Where there's pain and suffering, may my wounded body be your source of grace for others.

In that month, the disease had taken its toll on me. After nearly a hundred tests, appointments, and surgeries, my body, mind, and spirit had been transformed. I had become soft, calm, and highly sensitive. I cried easily.

I noticed these changed emotions while visiting a few friends living with cancer. When I stood or sat next to them, I felt their anguish. When I prayed for them, their sorrow was also my sorrow. So, I cried. At times, I wept externally and could taste my tears. At other times, I cried internally when I felt a sense of sadness.

In many ways, tears became water for my soul. They were tears of love. My experience of pain and suffering had given me a tender heart. So now, I am sensitive to my surroundings and pay more attention to others. I remember the words of the prophet Ezekiel: "I will remove the heart of stone from your flesh and give you a heart of flesh" (Ez 36:26).

Yes, I now have a new heart, wounded, hurt, and broken. But everyone hurts, and everyone weeps. Even Jesus wept. I have learned to accept whatever life gives me: joy and pain, sunshine and rain. My life has been enlightened by God's grace, my way of living illuminated by what I see and experience. I am grateful for that.

As for my pain and suffering, these are gifts to me, my source of grace. Maybe this is how God loves me tender, just like that Elvis Presley song; in his heart, I belong. My dreams have been fulfilled in you, my God. I love you, and I always will.

As I continue to fight cancer, there have been a lot of up-and-down moments. Each moment God is there, holding me tight. I have a new, tender heart, and it is a heart of grace and a heart of light. I am so blessed to live in this beautiful world that God has created for me. I am blessed to be one of his creatures with a tender heart.

Prayer

Grant me, O Lord my God, a mind to know you,
a heart to seek you, wisdom to find you, conduct

Tears of Love

pleasing to you, faithful perseverance in waiting for you, and a hope of finally embracing you.[1]

O Mary! My hope, please recommend me to your son Jesus, and obtain for me the grace to love your son wholeheartedly, especially in my time of sickness.

A Moment of Grace

By now, I hope to have convinced you that suffering is not evil and is for our benefit, a share in the Passion of Our Lord. How do you handle your suffering? Bearing it patiently with serenity and for the love of God, or bearing it irritated, impatient, resistant? If we take courage and bear our suffering for the Lord, we can experience God's grace and mercy in the form of his consolation.

Act of Surrender

Father, into your hands I commend my spirit.
—*Luke 23:46*

Through the gift of suffering, I receive the ability to endure, which strengthens my character. By surrendering my will, I come to trust God and let the Holy Spirit move me accordingly. This is not easy, but with God's grace I can come to him and surrender myself into his hands, just as Jesus surrendered himself from the Cross.

Through this act of surrender, I place myself in the hand of God joyfully, rather than out of simple resignation. I once overheard a friend asking my wife about me. She replied, "He is in the hand of God." At first, I was saddened by the hopeless tone of her words. I felt like a father holding his son's hand and then suddenly feeling the child yank his hand away. Her words fell hard upon my heart.

During my morning prayer, sitting alone at church, I looked at God the Father and said, "I am sorry." Then, without another word, I reached out to him. Together, we were back together again, hand in hand. It was an act of trust and of surrender.

Act of Surrender

Moments later, I felt teardrops on my face. Out of nowhere, I tasted the goodness of "being in the Father's hand." In a flickering second, time froze; I experienced the kingdom of God within me as I held God's hand. He was next to me, very much within my reach. Tearfully, I realized what was happening to me—*I was with Abba, my Father.*

I continued with my morning prayer in a mixture of joy and sorrow, until finally there were no more tears to shed. I was indeed in the arms of God, and he had turned my mourning into dancing. From that moment, I was content in dealing with my pain and sorrow. I freely accepted the will of God for me to be sick, for the sake of Abba.

As time went by, the results of my cancer treatments became a mixture of hope and disappointment, joy and pain, good and bad news. Each time I received dubious outcomes, I learned to return to the foot of the Cross and surrender myself to God. Especially when I am overwhelmed, I return there and I pull out a kind of white flag as a gesture of my surrender to God.

I need to stay focused on God alone. Outside of God, "all things are vanity" (Eccl 1:2). In many ways, I am grateful for the gift of suffering when my sorrow forces me to surrender to God's will. When I kneel down to pray, to weep, and to meet God, I don't need to see him in person, for he is within me. Faith and grace make it possible for me to be with God. He is a good Father who is the only one who can comfort my weary soul. I am happy to be in God's hands and surrender myself to him.

Prayer

O Jesus, I surrender myself to you. Take care of everything! *(Repeat this prayer ten times.)*[1]

"In you, LORD, I take refuge; let me never be put to shame. In your righteousness deliver me; incline your ear to me; make haste to rescue me.
Be my rock of refuge, a stronghold to save me. For you are my rock and my fortress; for your name's sake lead me and guide me.
Free me from the net they have set for me, for you are my refuge. Into your hands I commend my spirit; you will redeem me, LORD, God of truth" (Ps 31:1–6).

A Moment of Grace

Words have meaning and can hurt. Ask God for the grace to be attentive to how your words affect others. Ask him also to help you recognize your own vulnerability and not overreact to certain words, tones, and suggestions.

Being sick is a difficult task. But if we come to God often and create a sacred place, God can help us with our troubles. God is always there to care and listen and is ready to act. Are you ready to truly say, with your hearts as well as your lips, "O Jesus, I surrender myself to you"? I hope the answer is yes.

Facing Reality

You will know the truth, and the truth will
set you free.
—John 8:32

Through the gift of suffering, we are able to obtain the spirit of bravery and courage. Having cancer is painful, and eventually it may lead to death. No doubt, we may be afraid of pain and dying. To alleviate this fear, we must face our reality. Once we know the reality, we can act courageously, while asking for the grace to handle it gracefully.

Take courage in facing reality. Christ gives suffering a new meaning and a redemptive quality. Suffering for Christ also means suffering for his kingdom, which means suffering for others as well. This reality is scary, yet we must face it to achieve this kind of saving grace. This is true not only for us but also for those who love us.

In the Gospel of Matthew Jesus gives his followers—and gives to us as well—an example of how we can face reality: "We are going up to Jerusalem, and the Son of Man will be handed over to the chief priests and the scribes, and they will condemn him to death, and hand him over to the Gentiles to be mocked and scourged and crucified, and he will be raised on the third day" (Mt 20:18–19). He told them what was in store, revealed God's plan for them to see, and gave them courage. And so it is with us.

After years of countless treatments, my illness worsened, and I found myself facing a final option: chemotherapy. I was shaken by the news and wasn't sure how to react. Friends had talked about the horrible side effects of this treatment, but that was not what was bothering me the most. I was thinking about my mother. After seeing me doing well for a while, she had high hopes that I would recover. I didn't want to break her heart by telling her, "No, I am not doing well, Mother."

How can a son talk with his parents about his own impending, painful death? As I searched for the words to tell my parents about my cancer progression, I could not help but think of Jesus's first prediction of the Passion in Luke 9:22: that he must suffer greatly, and that he was going to die.

I wonder how Jesus told the Blessed Mother, and how she reacted to such a message? As Our Lady, "full of grace," she would have had everything she needed to handle any situation, including her son's ultimate sacrifice. But I was not so confident that my own mother had this strength, and I prayed for her to receive just "a drop of grace" to accept my fate and not be bitter or to despair.

Early one morning, as I contemplated what to say to my mother during my morning prayer before I went to church, I heard Jesus ask me, "Can you be sick for me?"

Looking up at the Cross, I replied, "Yes, Lord. You know that I will say yes, for I do not know how to say no."

Facing Reality

I wept, knowing the consequence of accepting the invitation. After Mass, I found the courage to tell my parents about my health condition. It was a drop of grace, and it solved all my troubles.

My mother listened and reacted to the news gracefully. She shared the news with everyone in my family. Once the rest of my family knew about my health condition, they could keep caring for me as I continued my journey. It's my job to be sick for the Lord, for my sweet Jesus, and for the sake of his sorrowful Passion, along with Our Lady. I know I am going to be fine.

Prayer

Remember, O most gracious Virgin Mary, that never was it known that anyone who fled to thy protection, implored thy help, or sought thine intercession was left unaided.

Inspired by this confidence, I fly unto thee, O Virgin of virgins, my mother; to thee do I come, before thee I stand, sinful and sorrowful. O Mother of the Word Incarnate, despise not my petitions, but in thy mercy hear and answer me. Amen.[1]

A Moment of Grace

Have you avoided sharing your suffering with others, to let others see your weakness? It's okay to be weak, even to the point of death. Is it difficult for you to let others care for you? Sickness is a great teacher of humility for both the sick and the caregiver.

When you are sick, do you show your trust in God by going to him, praying to him, asking him for what you need, thanking and praising him no matter what the outcome? It's up to God—to give or not to give. We need to present our desires to God, knowing that God fills the hungry with good things and lifts up the lowly because of their humility (see Luke 1:52–53). Thus, humility is a powerful gift; it moves God's heart.

The Way of Abandonment

> My God, my God, why have you forsaken me?
> —*Mark 15:34*

Through the gift of suffering, I discover the power of God's grace deep within me. Within this power, I find great strength to pick up my cross and follow Jesus. However, prior to this encounter, it seems that I must learn to detach, to let go of things. One method of this detachment is the way of abandonment. In doing so, the spirit of God can enter and fill up what is best for me. What the spirit gives is the power of God's grace, an inner strength.

In a time of sickness, particularly longanimity (long-suffering), the increase of pain often makes people feel abandoned. It seems to them like no one cares. But with God's grace and a little humility they learn to unite in their suffering with the suffering Christ, and this unity leads them to walk in the way of peace. Walking this way of peace is a form of strength; in it, I experience the power of God's grace deep within.

I speak from my experience. There are numerous occasions when I have felt abandoned. To survive, I learned to totally depend on God and not on anyone or anything materially. Here, I let go and "cast myself on the cross where the suffering Christ finds myself entirely." Without a doubt, this is an agonizing process and a painful experience, but it's good for me because I can let go of my will and my way of life. This is when the spirit of God can move me freely. It's a moment of grace when I can do God's will instead of my own.

In the school of suffering, feelings of abandonment can lead me to discover the meaning of detachment. By "letting go" of things, even of life itself, I gain more. I am able to follow Jesus, "For whoever wishes to save his life will lose it, but whoever loses his life for my sake will find it" (Mt 16:25).

When I started the chemotherapy medicine, no one from my family was with me. I was nervous and frightened knowing what I was about to face. No one was there for me to cry with, hold my hand, encourage my weary soul, or offer any consolation. When I got home, I was so upset that I didn't eat dinner. I ran to see a friend and unloaded my sorrow. I avoided the chapel, knowing that I would only cry like a baby to the Lord.

The next day, the heavy feelings lingered, and anger began to rise to the surface. During my morning prayer, while everyone was still sleeping, I burst out in a loud crying voice and I wept and wept. From the depths of my heart and soul, I cried out, "My Lord and my God." That was all I could pray.

Suddenly, I realized that going forward with this chemotherapy, I was going to face abandonment; I would be entering a narrow gate. As part of the "narrow gate" experience, I could not depend on human consolation and

The Way of Abandonment

companionship, including my family and friends. Instead, I had to learn to surrender to the mercy of God. It was my only hope.

Thanking the Lord for this heavenly wisdom, I stopped weeping and opened my breviary to start the Liturgy of the Hours. Each word and verse was like an electric shock to each beat of my heart and soul. I had never experienced this kind of prayer. It was then I felt my crying voice reach heaven. God was with me, and I was with God.

This experience boosted my confidence to move forward, knowing I had everything I needed. "The LORD is my strength" (Ps 28:7), and even though I walk through the valley of the shadow of death (cancer), I will fear no evil, for God is with me. He anoints my head with oil, and my cup overflows. Indeed, goodness and mercy will pursue me all the days of my life (see Psalm 23).

I knew more suffering was in store, yet I felt content. The more "bad things" happened, the closer I got to God. In the end, abandonment was not something I would have put on my list. But in the life of redemptive suffering, it's good to put it on the list.

Prayer

O Lord, sometimes it is hard to be a sick person. No word or action can ever mend a suffering body. I cannot escape it. Please, Lord, show me how to be sick since I cannot escape it. Therefore, I come sick to you, "the physician of life, as one unclean . . . poor and needy." Bless me with your tender compassion. Guide my feet into the way of peace.

Please shine on me like the dawn on high, breaking any darkness and mending any illness. Penetrate the inner core of my being. Be my source of strength, wisdom, peace, courage, and power. For I am in you, and you are in me.

Today I open my heart and soul to you, Lord. Please come to do your job as my Divine Physician. I, too, shall do my job—to hold on to hope, even as I am sick, for you. Whether I live or die, everything shall be under your control, and I will be okay so long as I am with you.

A Moment of Grace

Have you ever known a life situation that you thought was "very bad" but turned out to be "very good"? It happens more often than we think. This phenomenon teaches us to remain calm when facing difficult situations. On the surface it may look terrible. However, as time goes by, we may come to see things differently. Stay calm. Follow the way of detachment. Let go of the "snapping" moment; don't rush to judgment, and be patient.

Conversation with My Son

> I must die before I die. So, when I die, I have nothing to die for.
>
> —*St. John of the Cross*

One gift of suffering is the awareness of our own mortality, the certainty of death. To enter the gate of heaven, I must die here on earth.

Each person comes into the world differently. Likewise, each person shall leave this world distinctively. To prepare for my departure, I try to practice the words of St. John of the Cross to "die before I die" while I am still living. As part of my preparation, I also prepare for the one that I love.

As my condition worsened, I decided to share the news with my teenage son. We must all experience some suffering in life. I hoped this difficult dialogue would trigger or enhance his sense of empathy and compassion. If the Lord were to call me home, I did not want him to get upset at God.

So, I started the conversation. "You know what is happening to me?"

"Tell me," he replied. "Tell me, and don't sugarcoat it."

"I've got to start chemotherapy," I answered. "Cancer is eating up my bones. I get jaw pain and other side effects. Thus, I won't be able to do many things for you and with you, and I may die." I paused, and when he remained silent, I pressed a bit more. "How do you feel about what I just said?"

He got up, looked away from me, and said, "What am I going to do with mom and my sister when you're gone?" I didn't know what to say to him right away.

The next day, I spoke with him again. "Son, when I am gone, you shall take over my place. You shall be the man of this household. You're a man, you know. God gives each of us a role to play. As a man, I have already given you an example. If mom and your sister want something, do what you can to help them.

"Remember all the places that we visited and the things that we did together? Like me, you be there for them; you plan and take them there; you care for and protect them, and you must love and forgive them. More important, just love them for me." Again, there was a silence between us.

I did not want our conversation to end there, however. I wanted my son to hear directly from my lips about God's love. "I am sorry to have to talk to you in this way. Please do not blame God for my suffering or be angry at him. At my departure, if that day comes, I hope you would not walk away from God. Please know that I love God and he loves me." Again, there was a silence between us.

It had been a difficult conversation for both of us. But I felt a great sense of grace and blessing. I hoped to give my son an opportunity to let me go while I was still living.

Conversation with My Son

Together, we both can celebrate the gift of life, both in living and dying. I want him to go on with life and make his destiny as God wants him to do.

In the end, my greatest joy is to see him happy and discovering God. Whether I live or not, I shall be with him, and he shall be with me. I will always be his father, and he will always be my son.

As for my daughter, she was too young, and I didn't want to put this burden onto her. But somehow, I may already have done so.

Prayer

"Lord, teach us to count our days aright, that we may gain wisdom of heart" (Ps 90:12).

A Moment of Grace

Surely, it is very difficult to talk to our children about death and suffering. Despite that, I still think it's important to help our children learn about suffering, to teach them what suffering is, how to bear it, and how to receive benefits from any suffering. Use suffering as a teaching moment. Teach them how to accept suffering in their lives, how to ask God for help in times of trouble, and how to bring their suffering in union with the suffering Christ.

In this way, suffering for the love of Jesus is something that can bring great joy in life. By watching our example, our children can obtain the skill necessary to bear their own suffering—and to understand that God will always give them the strength they need to carry their suffering.

As you have come this far in reading these words of mine, I'm sure you agree that we all suffer in different ways and to different degrees, including physical, mental, emotional, moral, and intellectual. As I share with you about my suffering, you will learn from my experience. The gift of suffering teaches me that I must share my experience with others so that they can learn.

Battle Fatigue

> If the spirit of the one who raised Jesus from the dead dwells in you, the one who raised Christ from the dead will give life to your mortal bodies also, through his spirit that dwells in you.
>
> —*Romans 8:11*

Through the gift of suffering we obtain the power of Christ in us. One of the many reasons suffering is a great problem in human life is the lack of strength that comes with it. It makes a person fatigued, weak, and vulnerable. We all realize that modern medicine can ease and cure much sickness. However, it simply cannot take away suffering entirely.

This is why redemptive suffering plays an important part in the life of the believer who suffers. Christ gives us a new meaning to suffering. As I follow him and remain in union with him, I can obtain the same spirit of God that was in Jesus (see Romans 8:11). This verse implies that we have the same power to carry our cross just as Jesus did. Here is how I discovered the power of Christ within me.

As the fatigue caused by chemotherapy intensified, I could operate only at a bare minimum of my capacity.

My voice slowly faded away until I couldn't talk. I developed blisters on my hands and feet and experienced many other adverse events. All these were side effects of the chemotherapy treatment.

However, I refused to let sickness win the battle. Pain is a great battle of the body, mind, and spirit. And as the pain rattled my body, I decided to strike back by getting out of the house and cleaning the yard that had been neglected.

At first, I couldn't do it. After taking a few steps outside, I was sweaty and tired. Fifteen minutes later, I was on the ground and I couldn't move. With my last bit of strength, I closed my eyes, lifted my spirit to almighty God, and called out, "Lord, help me to discover the power of Christ within me."

My prayer was like a megaphone that reached heaven. I got up and continued to work. Four hours later, I was able to finish half of what I wanted to do. So, I rested as the fatigue lingered. Then I continued to pray for the power of Christ within me; that was my prayer. That night, I rested well in the loving arms of my sweet Jesus.

The next day, Friday, was the Feast of the Sacred Heart of Jesus. When I got up early in the morning and took my medicines, I noticed something different: I felt normal. I wasn't tired like many previous days. Instead, I felt a refreshing, great feeling from within. Power overflowed in my body, and I felt strong like never before. It was indeed the power of Christ within me. This power restored my voice and took away my fatigue so I could do what I needed to do.

So, what did I do with that power? I went to church to thank God for making me strong. I was so strong that I drove three hours to Charlotte to see my family. I missed them and had wanted to see them since Christmas, but I couldn't because I was too weak and too sick. I spent three hours visiting them. Afterward, I drove straight back home on the same day. It was another three hours on the road. In total, I spent six hours on the road. For a person who was on chemotherapy and had to deal with side effects, six hours of driving was a heroic act because it was simply an impossible task. Yet with the power of Christ anything is possible, for nothing is impossible.

On my way home, I thought about St. Joan of Arc. She said, "Act, and God will act."[1] On that day, I received the power of God within me by acting on what I had received. In doing so, God allowed me to experience his power within me, the power that made me feel alive again. The power let me rejoice and be glad. I thank God for giving me the gift of Christ's power within me.

Prayer

Lord, help me to discover the power of Christ within me, all the days of my life.

A Moment of Grace

"Willpower" is a gift from God. It's the mental intellect that convinces us to do what needs to be done. We must exercise our minds, like we exercise our bodies, to be strong and productive.

Without this discipline, the mind lacks self-control and self-confidence and is subject to our moods and whims.

If the mind is not strong, it will likely go along with what the body wants and not put up a fight. For example, my body may tell me to stay home, be lazy, and do nothing. Sometimes, that is fine. Other times, I may need to will to get up and do something to avoid falling into despair and sadness.

In your time of sickness, can your mind put up a fight? What can you do so that you don't fall into despair?

Ask God for grace so you can persist in willing your body, mind, and spirit.

When God Speaks Forgiveness

> He will wipe every tear from their eyes, and
> there shall be no more death or mourning,
> wailing or pain, [for] the old order has passed
> away.
>
> —*Revelation 21:4*

To experience redemptive suffering is to participate in the work of forgiveness—both the giving and receiving of it. Even though I have suffered, I have also received God's consolation on numerous occasions, including one holy experience that let me know that God has forgiven my sins.

One early morning pain woke me up. Each heartbeat felt like a tiny needle poking at my heart from behind my back. I had felt this pain before, and I knew what I must do. I recognized that it was the cancer pain, an irresistible force that induced me to stop everything, including sleeping, to pay attention to my body.

When this kind of pain occurs, I have learned that I need to run to the foot of the Cross and pray to the suffering Christ. That morning, I got up early and decided to go to church, even though I was in pain. It was the Feast of the Immaculate Heart of Mary, and so I placed myself in the presence of Mary and Jesus's hearts. At Mass, I placed myself in the company of Mary's heart and the Sacred Heart of Jesus.

As I sat there throughout the Mass, offering my heart to the Lord and Our Lady, out of nowhere came a gentle voice, whispering in the very depth of my heart, and I heard this inner voice say, *"Your sins are forgiven."*

In a split second, I was struck with awe and mesmerized by this eternal voice. The message was loud and clear that Jesus had forgiven my sins. I was fully alert, my mind was cleared, my eyes were opened, I was not taking narcotic medications that caused my mind to hallucinate, and my conscience was aware of my surroundings; the experience was like hearing the voice of the spirit of God.

Though I could not find words and expressions to fully describe this holy encounter, I simply knew that my sins have been forgiven by God. I felt a profoundly deep love of God for me. A rain of grace poured down on me on that day. That moment, I was like the prodigal son received by the great love of the Father (see Luke 15:11–32). Oh! What a feeling to be loved by the great Father. I was in the arms of the great Father. It was an indescribable feeling.

Prayer

"O Most Blessed Mother, heart of love, heart of mercy, ever listening, caring, consoling, hear our prayer. . . . We are comforted in knowing your heart is ever open to those who ask for your prayer. We trust to your gentle care and intercession those whom we love and who are sick or lonely or hurting. Help all of us, Holy Mother, to bear our burdens in this life until we may share eternal life and peace with God forever.

Amen."[1]

A Moment of Grace

The best way to receive forgiveness of sin is through the Sacrament of Reconciliation. When was the last time you went to Confession? In a time of sickness, it is essential to be in a state of grace and be prepared for death. After Confession we are in the state of grace. If the Lord calls us home, we need to be ready to go to meet him. Why not speak with your priest today? Come and receive the Sacraments of Anointing of the Sick and Reconciliation.

Suffering Is a Sign

> If God sends you many sufferings, it is a sign
> he has great plans for you.
> —*St. Ignatius of Loyola*

Suffering is a sign that God wants us to obtain the gift of his consolation in a unique way. Many times we fail to recognize this consolation as a gift. Maybe it's because we don't know how to suffer well or are unable to see that suffering builds character. Perhaps we fail to see suffering as an opportunity for others to show love or as a funnel of grace and joy as we offer our sufferings for the spiritual benefit of others.

Some people only see suffering as a bad sign, related to evil, weakness, sin, or punishment. Their pain obscures their own vision of God. But when we see suffering as a sign of God's desire to work in us, suffering becomes a sign of hope, love, peace, grace, mercy, pardon, and glory.

To see that suffering is a sign of God's providential care, I must learn to be patient and vigilant in handling my suffering. I find the following five elements to be helpful.

Suffering Is a Sign

First, I must ask the Holy Spirit for counsel. I must ask God to teach me to understand my options, give me wisdom in the situation, and strengthen me to act.

Second, I go to Our Lady of Sorrows and ask her to pray to Jesus for me and obtain for me a special grace that allows me to receive God's consolation.

Third, I pray to the Communion of Saints, asking them to favor me with their intercessions. If you have a favorite saint, this is the moment to pray to them. Here are some favorite saints of mine: I frequently turn to St. Peregrine as the patron saint for cancer patients, to St. Bernadette for healing, to St. Thomas Aquinas for wisdom, to St. Paul for strength, to St. Peter for faithfulness, to St. Padre Pio for prayers, and many others.

Fourth, I pray to the suffering Christ. He is calling us to "come to me, all you who labor and are burdened, and I will give you rest" (Mt 11:28). Christ invites us to unite with him on the Cross and receive the glory of the Resurrection with him.

Fifth, I do penance and go to Confession on a regular basis. It's here where we receive God's mercy and pardon. I believe in doing these five elements, we will see that suffering is a sign of God's love, grace, peace, and consolation.

Prayer

O Lord, my God, I have a great fear of being sick. But let my fear be a divine fear. Teach me to run to you at the heart of my sickness and not away from you. This way, my sickness shall be my cross, and it does not produce bitterness. Instead, it sparks a deep love for you.

Please draw my weary spirit into your heart, lead me to stretch out my arms, and give me all-embracing love, as you did on the Cross. Lord, have mercy on me and let me present my body as a living sacrifice, and all that I am as an offering to you that may be acceptable.

Lord, may my fear of death be my birth to a new life in heaven. Let me put on the garment of grace and the cross on my forehead as your protection. On my knees, I shall burn the sweet-smelling incense of prayer continually. With full confidence in you, O Lord, here I am as a living sacrifice. I know you desire not death, but faith; you thirst not for pain and suffering, but self-surrender; and you desire mercy above all.

Thank you, Lord, for loving me, just the way I am.

A Moment of Grace

When we face difficulty and hardship, can we treat them as moments of grace? With a life rooted in prayer, let us humbly ask the Lord: "God, come to my assistance. Lord, make haste to help me." Remember, God loves to fill the hungry with good things and to lift the lowly.

Do not be afraid in times of sickness, hardship, trial, and tribulation. Take courage, put up a holy fight, and run the race to win. Take your

Suffering Is a Sign

troubles to the foot of the Cross and be grateful always, especially in your spiritual trials and your heartbreaks. The first-class seating, the front row in paradise, is for those with a grateful spirit.

Go to Our Lady of Sorrows

> Behold, your mother.
> —*John 19:27*

When you are suffering, go to Our Lady, Mother of Mercy, our greatest and most compassionate advocate. When we ask Our Lady for her intercession, she obtains for us the gift of God's consolation.

Our Lady of Sorrows understands the extent of human suffering, for she went through the Passion with Christ. Beginning with the Prophecy of Simeon (see Luke 2:34–35), Our Lady understood that her heart would be pierced by a sword. Thus, she merits an intimacy with God unlike any other creature. Therefore, God reveals things to her that he does not reveal to others.

From the Cross, our Savior gave Our Lady to the world (see John 19:27). With that, the suffering Christ allows us to petition her so that she may reveal hidden things to us. When sorrow weighs us down, we can turn to Our Lady of Sorrows and ask her to give us a helping hand.

In my long-suffering struggle with cancer, I initially had difficulty facing the truth about the future of my life, now filled with severe pain, side effects, and even death. I

Go to Our Lady of Sorrows

dreaded sharing this sorrowful news with my family. So, I went to Our Lady of Sorrows and asked her to help me.

My mother. I had a holy conversation with my mother. When I was a year old, I contracted polio that paralyzed both of my legs. My mother spent much of her fortune seeking medical care for me. More recently, she shared with me her agony in seeing me suffering. She said, "I don't know what I did that God punished me by making you a crippled child, and now cancer."

Of course, her pain is my pain; and, I am sure, my pain is God's pain as well. But praise God, for he heals the broken hearts and binds up their sorrows (see Psalm 147:3). As I listened to my mother and her words of pain, I remembered the words of Jesus: "Neither he nor his parents sinned; it is so that the works of God might be made visible through him" (Jn 9:3). My mother had suffered many sleepless nights at the thought of me and my suffering. She had asked the Lord for healing so many times, but so far, nothing.

She asked God over and over, Why I must be the one of her six children who suffers the most? From a childhood of polio, to fourteen years of family separation, surgery after surgery, and now cancer. Why? Why? Why? She sighed.

As she asked her questions aloud, all I could do was sit and listen and pray for wisdom. At last, I answered, "Maybe it's because God loves me. Maybe I am like gold and silver in the melting pot, to get tested and purified by fire. God purifies and disciplines those he loves. Maybe I am truly loved by God. I know that I am a sinner, and I need to be disciplined. The sicker I am, the humbler I become. Please don't worry about a thing like cancer. Be fearful of what can kill both body and soul. God alone can save us."

I stopped, and there was silence between us. "Mom," I continued, "next time, when you find it hard to sleep, you say this prayer, then everything will be all right: "Lord, I thank you for loving my son more than I love him."

My mom laughed gently. "I kept asking him to heal you," she said. "I forgot to give him thanks and praise. I will do what you told me next time." With that, I felt peace knowing God will make all things right.

I thank Our Lady of Sorrows for allowing me to have this holy conversation with my mother. I am confident in her advocacy, and whenever I am sad I come to her and receive her consolation. She's always there to help me.

Prayer

O Mary, Mother of God, I come to you sinful and sorrowful, by your grace; help me to make my inconsolable grief an eternal offering to your son, our Lord and Savior. Teach me to know Jesus and come to him for rest, for his yoke is easy and his burden light. O Mary, let me come to you as well, more and more, because through you is through Jesus. Grant me your grace with your sacred heart, so I can intimately unite to you and to Jesus, heart to heart and light to light, a perfect harmony.

Go to Our Lady of Sorrows

A Moment of Grace

Life is full of incomprehensible mystery. Sometimes, it is all right to ask a question. Asking is a way to "ponder" and "reflect" on the things that we do not understand. Our Lady pondered a few times in her heart (see Luke 1:29 and Luke 2:19, 51). With a humble heart we, too, can ponder these unknown events that are difficult to face.

Those who ponder God love the wisdom of God. In fact, one of the five remedies for sorrow is to contemplate truth. St. Thomas Aquinas states, "The contemplation of truth assuages pain or sorrow, and the more so, the more perfectly one is a lover of wisdom."[1] When you face a difficulty and cannot find the answer, can you accept what is unknown and turn it into a source of wisdom with help from God?

Becoming God's "Love Dumpster"

> You are rewarded not according to your work or your time but according to the measure of your love.
>
> —*St. Catherine of Siena*

Through the gift of suffering we receive the opportunity for others to show love. This love transcends into God's love where both the giver and receiver praise God. Like the parable of the Good Samaritan (see Luke 10:25–37), we get to experience God's love dumpster, where both the giver and receiver give and receive love.

About God's love dumpster. As I carry my cross in battling cancer, I can connect with other people who share their pain and suffering with me. As Graceman, I become God's love dumpster, where people come and release their anguish onto me. It is an honor to be God's love dumpster because it reminds me that my suffering is not in vain. It is a source of grace for others.

Not long ago, I knelt before the Holy Eucharist, and I pondered the image of being God's love dumpster. How was it possible that my wounded body has slowly become a source of grace for others? Of course, I am just an instrument. I am not sure how this unfolded, but I trust the work of the Holy Spirit that continues to move me to do his will. I will continue to pray to be moved by the Holy Spirit and accept to be God's instrument. To be God's love dumpster is to discover that "when I am weak, then I am strong" (2 Cor 12:10).

At home, I stand in front of a mirror and see the man in it. I am wounded and broken in so many aspects of my life. Yet, I am loved by God, and the love of God moves me to do his holy will. So, I become God's love dumping ground. People come and shower me with their love. In return, what I receive, I give to those who need love, hope, and peace. The Holy Spirit uses my wounded body as a source of grace for others.

As for me, standing by the mirror, I see that this is my time to be sick with cancer. I see that the love of God is in me. So, I am at peace and joyfully accept this thorn in my flesh. With God's grace, I shall learn about this new season of mine. It has changed from health to sickness, and I am at peace in this new season. Whatever comes my way, I shall embrace it, even being a dumpster. Whether sickness or health, pain or joy, weakness or strength, rich or poor, living or dying, "I have the strength for everything through him who empowers me" (Phil 4:13). I am content to be broken and wounded for the sake of Christ. And I am fully confident in the mercy God has for me.

So, bring it on, for I am Graceman.

Prayer

Lord, may I live to glorify you. May my wounded body be your source of grace for others.

A Moment of Grace

We are all handicapped. Each of us has a physical "thorn in the flesh" that may make us uncomfortable, something we just wish would go away. Perhaps it is something about our appearance, or some chronic weakness or sickness. Whatever form your "thorn in your flesh" takes, take that, and ask God for grace. Then you, too, can say, "When I am weak, then I am strong."

The Blessing of Chronic Illness

> I consider that the sufferings of this present
> time are as nothing compared with the glory
> to be revealed for us.
>
> —*Romans 8:18*

To receive the gift of suffering is to wholly surrender to the mercy of God. For more than fifty years, I have been living with serious illness—first polio, then cancer. Through faith, I have recognized that my sickness is a blessing in disguise. I thank the Lord for allowing me to share his Passion as I carry these crosses. By the grace of God, I have come to see that my sickness is the work of the Holy Spirit that has been made visible through me.

First, I joyfully accept being "sick for the Lord." This is my season to be sick so that God's glory can be visible. Naturally, I do not *want* sickness to happen to me or anyone. I despise being sick. I am tired of it. It's painful, humiliating, beating me to death, and I could go on complaining and whining all day long about being sick. If I had a choice, I would surely and certainly refuse to be sick. But this is wishful thinking.

So instead, I face my sickness gracefully. I can be bitter, or I can be better. As Graceman, I want to be better always and let the joy of the Gospel of suffering be heard. As a result, I received God's consolation, and I am writing about it so that people may find hope in God. Finding hope in times of sickness is the joy of the Gospel of suffering.

Second, God's grace is visible in that I can preach without preaching. When I walk with a disability, people appreciate that they have two great legs, whereas I don't. I hope they will stop and thank God for that. As people watch me battle cancer, I hope they thank God for the gift of health and use it for the glory of God. I hope my disability causes people to live out virtues like love, kindness, and mercy toward others.

When I was young, I thought of polio as a curse, and I avoided looking at myself, feeling shame. Now that I am older, I know God certainly makes up for what is lacking. Being sick, I don't have good health. But I am okay because I have other gifts to make up for it. What I lack here, I shall receive as a great reward when I am in heaven. With disability, I must think outside the box. Thus, my disability is my ability to live gracefully.

Third, because of my illness, I see the beauty of the cross and the grace overflowing from it. Surely, I am unattractive because of my walking disability and sickness. I get it. Now, I am poor in health and slow in thinking and acting because of my "chemo brain." But I am rich in many ways. I may be slow, but I won't give up. Sometimes, I am lost and confused, but I'm not giving up on hope. I have learned to become a great hope hunter. As for my cross, it hurts, but it always heals. Friends who know me

The Blessing of Chronic Illness

know that my courage and fortitude are the derivatives of enduring hardships. I am Graceman precisely because of the way I live my life and handle obstacles.

In short, the Gospel is largely about suffering. Out of that, suffering is conquered by love. Thus, the Gospel is also about love. In my time of suffering, the love of God is made brightly visible because I learn to surrender and allow the mercy of God to illuminate my suffering. My sickness is my blessing indeed.

Prayer

Thank you, God, for the gift of life. Thank you for the grace that helps me not to be bitter, but to be better. Thank you for my sickness, a blessing in disguise, that makes your grace visible through me. Let me shine your light, so that people will see you in me as I simply walk through life.

A Moment of Grace

With grace, all things are possible. It's through faith that I discover the power of grace. So, I hope you all will take time to build up your faith while you're still strong and healthy. Hopefully, you will obtain God's grace so that you can bear your cross in your time of sickness. Even with my crosses, I still have a great life. I hope you will too. Be strong, and count your blessings.

The Desert of Redemptive Suffering

> Let all men know that grace comes after tribulation . . . This is the only true stairway to paradise, and without the cross they can find no road to climb to heaven.
>
> —*St. Rose of Lima*

It has been four years that I have been fighting cancer and nearly two years since I started chemotherapy, which tries to strip away my humanity. Even the pleasure of eating and drinking has slowly dissipated. Everything tastes like salt. My voice comes and goes throughout the day. My energy level is up and down. My bones start to crack and break. The hospital is like my second home. And night after sleepless night, I am tempted to fall into despair because all the side effects of treatment are like physical thorns in my flesh.

Thankfully, I am not sick to the point that I must stay in bed all day. Yet many times I cannot work because I am sick. In these moments I feel most vulnerable and emotional, like I'm riding on a roller coaster. And because I am not well enough for visitors, even to be around my family,

The Desert of Redemptive Suffering

I am alone frequently. This experience is like going to a desert with no entertainment, no purpose, and no direction. I am living, but it feels like I am dying. I still do small things, but it feels like I am doing nothing. I have time, but it seems I have no time. It is a changing season where I am tempted to fall into despair. Nevertheless, this is also the most sacred, holy, and peaceful time of my life.

One day, I drove myself to church, alone. There, I sat and wept. As my tears dried up, I got into my car and drove with no destination in mind. Though I was hungry, I couldn't eat much because I had lost my appetite due to chemotherapy. Then, fatigue kicked in. I stopped the car, rested in the parking lot of a Wendy's, and slept in the car. Shortly after, I got up, drove home, and continued to hide from my family.

This sense of helplessness opened a discovery for me, a beautiful lesson about faith and grace in suffering. When I am not feeling strong and turn to God for a helping hand, he always comes to my assistance in vast and various ways, even when driving on the road to nowhere. His faithfulness is my stronghold.

In all, I learned about the gift of peace. God is the giver of peace, so I come often to him for peace. And when I am with him, I let him do whatever he wants to me. If I feel like crying, I cry. If I just want to sit quietly with no book, no rosary, totally blank, then so be it. Whatever it is, I am content, emptying myself to be alone with God. Whenever I come to be with Jesus, I receive the gift of peace. I am in union with the suffering Christ. I am joined to him on the Cross. Pain is what we share. With that said, though I am sick, I am sick for the Lord, in him, through him, and with him.

Prayer

Lord, I give you my life. When I am sick and lonely, I turn my thoughts to you. Be with me and guide my feet into the way of peace.

O Mary! My hope, please help me to bear my burdens with grace. Please pray to Jesus for me.

A Moment of Grace

What is your understanding of peace? Like the prayer of peace by St. Francis, can you write your own prayer of peace? Can you be an instrument of peace for yourself? Where there is despair, you'll bring hope.

Part Four
The Way to New Life

> It is not by sidestepping or fleeing from suffering that we are healed, but rather by our capacity for accepting it, maturing through it and finding meaning through union with Christ, who suffered with infinite love.
>
> —*Pope Benedict XVI,* Spe Salvi (On Christian Hope*)*

It has been four years since I was diagnosed with stage four thyroid cancer. As I shared in the previous chapter, I don't have cancer. I only have this one big cross. My cross is my cancer, which has become the "one key" I carry daily. To my amazement, I have found this one key to be helpful. The one key becomes the master key with which I can open and close many doors, both big and small. Ultimately, I hope this master key will also unlock the vault of heaven.

Looking back on my life, I used to have many keys, and I was proud to have those keys. Each of those keys represented many aspects and accomplishments at different stages of my life. But now, I must put those keys away. It would be foolish to put many keys into my pocket when I have a big cross on my shoulder. I must carry this big cross of mine. If I don't, the weight of this big cross will crush me to death. This is the way to my new life. And with this new life, I have learned to consult not my fear but my hopes and my dreams. I shall think not about my frustrations but about my unfulfilled potential. I shall concern myself not with what I tried and failed in but with what is still possible for me to do. I want to keep and practice these great words of wisdom from St. John XXIII. So, what does the way to new life look like?

A new life always begins with a mother. She gives birth to a new life, and her infant child depends on her tender care. Without a mother life may not be possible, or at least, it isn't easy to survive without one. So far, it's truly been a great blessing to write about redemptive suffering and union with Jesus Christ. But to know Jesus is to know the Virgin Mary. She is the Mother of God and the Queen of Heaven. To unite with Jesus is to unite with her. It's to Jesus through Mary, according to St. Louis Marie de Montfort.

Jesus gives Mary to the world. "Behold your mother" (Jn 19:27). As a mother with many children in the world, she has many faces that her children can identify. As I am a Catholic Vietnamese-American, I have two images of her. She is Our Lady of Lourdes and Our Lady of Lavang.

In a previous chapter, I talked about Our Lady of Lourdes. Through her, I obtained the grace to face my suffering in a redemptive quality. The notion of being "sick for the Lord" became my source of grace. By her grace and through redemptive suffering, I received the gift of healing, endurance, preparation for death, and many others. But before all of these, I must go back to the source. It's the

Part Four: The Way to New Life

root of my birth to be able to identify Mary as Our Lady of Lavang.

The story of Our Lady of Lavang. The Reformation era gave birth to Catholicism in Vietnam. From its earliest days, the Church in Vietnam faced horrific persecutions. And so, to console her Vietnamese children, Our Lady appeared to them in the rainforest of Lavang. I will explore more in depth in the last chapter.

As for me, when the prospect of having cancer terrorized me and made me timid, I ran back to the "rainforest of Lavang" in my heart. Oh, I am still sick. So, I now come to Our Lady to tell her, "*Mẹ ơi!* (Mother dearest), the one you love is sick. It is I, the one you love who is sick."

I have learned to be with the suffering Christ. I shall learn to be with Our Lady of Lavang as well. She looks like me, a Vietnamese person; she speaks my language and knows how to shelter me from fear. I am sick, poor, and needy. I need her tender care. With my new life, I have come to know and love Our Lady of Lavang, a gentlewoman who looks like a Vietnamese, and she's my mother.

In the past, I could have done a better job in loving Our Lady as I should have. Now, I come sinful and sorrowful; I ask Our Lady to forgive me for being an ungrateful child. Like any good mother, I know she welcomes me back and loves me unconditionally. With my mother beside me—and like any son—I ask her to grant me the grace to endure trials and tribulations. The gift of endurance is the gift of healing. I know healing can come in many forms. Looking at Our Lady, I ask to receive the gift of God's consolation. Out of love, I place my confidence in the hands of Our Lady, for I know what I ask, I shall receive.

In my redemptive suffering, I know the suffering Christ gave Mary a special motherhood over all the people of the world. Just as she was the Mother of God in his suffering, so too she shall be for me and all humans in our suffering. She will teach me to unite with the suffering Christ. My suffering shall be a source of joy in this regard. It continues to allow me to have deep thoughts and conversations and create more opportunities for growth and spiritual heroism.

Finally, on the day of the ultimate redemption, Jesus shall wipe away the tears from my face and all faces. He shall reach out his hand for me to hold him tight. With my right hand, I am in the hand of God. Standing next to me is Mary, the Mother of God. I smile because she's my mother as well. Without hesitation, she, too, reaches out her hand so that my left hand can take her hand. On that day, I shall hear the voice of Jesus saying to me, "Today you will be with me in Paradise" (Lk 23:43).

With that, it's finished. I am in heaven.

Prayer

Mother of God, pray for me, a poor sinner.[1]

A Moment of Grace

The gift of suffering helps a person to reflect on the meaning of life in a holistic way. It is good to

Part Four: The Way to New Life

go back home again; it's the home of our childhood where we first received an abundance of joy, happiness, love, peace, and purpose. It was the age of our innocence, and somehow, time took it away. Still, it is possible to return to innocence again and see God's footprints in the sand as he was holding us up in our times of trouble. Knowing this, I hope we can truly praise the Lord and thank God eternally for the gift of the Father's grace.

The End of the Road

> Death is a passage from corruption to incorruption, from mortality to immortality, from troubles to tranquility.
>
> —*St. Ambrose*

With or without cancer, I am going to die. The road of life must end, and it's always difficult and fearful knowing that I must die. Dying is not an easy concept to accept. Nevertheless, it's an undeniable reality. Thus, I must ask God and Our Lady for special grace to accept this fact, stay calm, and remain faithful at the hour of death. I pray to St. Joseph for a peaceful death. For now, I ask Our Lady to obtain a special grace of holy perseverance, patience to endure, and the gift of preparation for death.

Living with cancer, death often visits me on my bed of suffering. It's always a terrifying moment. Thankfully, one of the gifts of long-suffering is that I have learned to deal gracefully with death. Over the years I have learned not to get frantic when the bell of death rings. Having faith lifts my fear so that I can be mindful of death without falling into panic. Then, I can be patient and properly prepare for death. It's through holy perseverance that I can achieve this wisdom.

The End of the Road

On one occasion, I felt hopeless thinking I would die. After seventeen months of chemotherapy, the severe side effects forced me to stop the treatment. Suddenly, I felt a sense of hopelessness because there weren't any more drugs available to help me. For years, I'd been talking about death. But now, it seemed that my journey was truly nearing the end. I was scared.

I am no longer like I used to be. I am older now, and it is becoming harder and harder to adjust, adapt, and accept anything new and uncertain. At this point, "to be sick for the Lord" means death. I am frightened and surely not ready to die. I'm in my early fifties, and I have two young children. I am old but not too old. Thus, the thought of dying causes my spirit to tremble and tremble. There are many sleepless nights when I fall into a pit of sadness, sorrowful, lonely, desolated, frail, and fragile. Thankfully, despite these weary nights, faith comes to my rescue, inspiring me to remain faithful to my Christian life. My sickness and fragility are not the time to walk away from my faith. Instead, my faith and way of life illuminate and intensify in knowing that I will die soon.

The thought of dying is now my cross. To carry my cross, I must look at Jesus on his Cross and Our Lady standing there next to him. Looking at him, I contemplate his pain with my pain. Seeing him suffering, I see that he's innocent, holy, and righteous. But out of obedience to the Father and the love for sinners, he dies. In this, I experience a deep sense of God's love, peace, and mercy.

As for Our Lady, I turn to her and ask her to pray for me, to obtain a special grace so I can remain calm in my time of sorrow.

Staying calm in a time of calamity and distress is spiritual heroism. One day when I am at the end of my rope, I hope and pray that in God's mercy he shall come and scoop me away from this valley of tears and welcome me home in heaven. With words of wisdom from St. Ambrose, I see death as "a passage from corruption to incorruption, from mortality to immortality, from troubles to tranquility."[1] I am at peace to be at the end of the road, for now.

Prayer

"Lord, now you let your servant go in peace; your word has been fulfilled: my own eyes have seen the salvation which you have prepared in the sight of every people: a light to reveal you to the nations and the glory of your people Israel."[2]

O, Mary! My hope and my Blessed Mother, obtain for me a seat in heaven where I can gaze at the inaccessible light of your son, my Redeemer. I thank you eternally for hearing and answering me. Amen.

A Moment of Grace

Are you tired to the point that you want to give up? Please don't give up. Please continue to take courage, run to the finish line, and claim the crown

The End of the Road

of victory. Ask God for the strength to bear your present troubles.

When we are tempted to give up, God always shows us a way out. Be humble and ask God for help. If you're in distress, look at the suffering Christ and turn your thoughts to him. He will take care of you.

Be patient in your asking. Impatience is a self-inflicted wound that only adds to the distress. But where there is pain, may you find God's grace. Where there is sorrow, may you experience God's consolation. Where there is sadness, may you be healed. Where there is trial and tribulation, may you empty yourself to God's will. Where there is doubt, may you trust in God's providential care. I pray that you shall find rest, peace, hope, and strength.

A New Kind of Love

> To love suffering and affliction out of love for
> God is the summit of most holy charity.
>
> —*St. Francis de Sales*

Suffering through sickness has allowed me to experience great love, mingled with kindness and compassion. Through this, I have also discovered a new meaning of love. I have learned that I must suffer to know what love is. Even if I must die, I should not be afraid, bitter, or despairing. The more I suffer, the more love I shall know. With love, I have everything. Without love, I am nothing.

There's a saying that money cannot buy love. All the wealth in the world will be useless when I die. However, love is its own currency through the gift of charity. Charity is one of the three theological virtues that inspires me to give without counting the cost. It also chases away many of my sins, such as bitterness, depression, and anger.

Charity fills me with love, teaching me to give without expecting a return. It's in giving that I receive a hundredfold in profit. So, when trials and tribulations, pain, and suffering are at my door, love is there too. When sickness strikes, I receive great love. It's the love from the people

A New Kind of Love

that love and care for me. In that love, I come to see God's love in me.

Love in a time of sickness serves as a great strength. It's that spirit that allows me to face my illness faithfully. Love is a remedy to cure my anguish, misery, sorrow, and hopelessness. Love can even conquer suffering. To receive this love, I must give love. I reap what I sow. The gift of charity is where I reap and sow.

Additionally, I also experience another kind of special gift in suffering. It's the gift of being able to "slow" the pace of life. Slowing down is a blessing in disguise because it forces me to see life's true colors. We live in a fast-moving society with a lot of distractions. If we don't intentionally make time for ourselves or God, we won't know how to love, how to live, how to listen, how to pray, how to cry, how to suffer, and even how to die. But now that I am sick, I have time to learn about these things wholeheartedly.

The gift of suffering allows me to change my way of life. With God's grace, my sickness enables me to embrace love. This love is so powerful that it has a healing effect: it takes away suffering, changes the heart, removes fear, and gives love to others.

With that kind of love, I have everything, and it shall be mine to keep for eternity. Not even death could take that love away. Nothing can separate me from that kind of love.

Prayer

Lord, thank you eternally for loving me like there are no others. Thank you truly for making me the apple of your eye. Thank you gracefully for the gift of life and for having faith to look for you. Finding you is the joy and love of my life.

A Moment of Grace

How do you define love in a time of sickness?

Patience in Dying

> Yes, I'm like a tired and harassed traveler,
> who reaches the end of his journey and falls
> over. Yes, but I'll be falling into God's arms!
>
> —*St. Thérèse of Lisieux*

Each of us comes into the world quite uniquely. So, too, we shall die quite distinctively. Thus, we can read, talk, write, and obtain all the knowledge about dying; then, we wait until death comes, and everything we obtained is turned upside down. However, patience alleviates fear.

Staying calm is one of the attributes of patience. With that said, is it possible that cancer can teach us a lot about the virtue of patience, how to die, and preparing to face death? I would like to think so.

After two years of chemotherapy, the cancer has multiplied in more places in my body. I am out of treatment options. I hope to continue living for as long as possible. For the sake of my family, I dream of remaining faithful to them. Sure, it's easier said than done. Regardless, it is always good to have hopes and dreams.

All my life I've been living with polio, a disability, and I could still move around. But now, chemotherapy's side effects are so brutal that I can hardly move. In addition, fatigue and other adverse effects impede my fragile body, including my thinking and doing. I must stop the treatment soon. So, sitting here, I find myself a bit weary because the bell of death has started to ring again. I said I was not afraid to die, but it seems I was lying. So now, I am trembling and trembling.

There are moments when I think I am ready to depart, yet I am not. I am scared, but not really. I am still living, but it seems I am dying. Dying is easy, but getting there is hard. I am sick, but I am as healthy as I can be. I am weak and tired, yet I am stronger than ever. I am so strong that I can endure and find enough courage to get up daily to live gracefully despite all the pain and suffering.

People say, "Take one day at a time." I interpret that as being patient and staying calm. These days, I am learning to do little things with love, trying to be faithful to the life that I know.

So here I am, trying to be a devoted father and husband while enduring what I must and remaining faithful to my Catholic beliefs. Despite my sleeplessness, I am still taking my kid to and from school and swimming practice at 5:30 a.m. I am active in my new "ministry of the present," meaning I am just there for my family to see that I am still living among them. I try not to complain much, for life is still beautiful. Yes, life is beautiful because it has come full circle, filled with ups and downs, health and sickness, joy and pain, crying and laughter, living and slowly dying. I taste them all.

Suddenly, the book of life is brief, time becomes precious, and the moment of grace opens wide. Thus, I must

Patience in Dying

live differently now. Slowly I am discovering how to let go of myself because everything I say or do seems contradictory and insufficient. This frustration may be how I can genuinely surrender and let God direct my pathway.

At times, I cry, hungry and thirsting for God's mercy. I beg the Lord to have mercy on my weary soul. I go to church more and more. Going there, I cast all my sorrows onto the suffering Christ and Our Lady. Here in this sacred place, tears have become my daily bread. It helps me cleanse my soul from emotional pain. When my tears dry up and I am ready to go home, I notice the anxiety has already departed, and the fear has dispersed into the air. What remains in me is the gift of peace, given to me by the mercy of God and the Mother of Mercy. With peace, I can be patient in dying.

Because I am still writing, it means death has not arrived. So, to be patient in dying is to love God and my neighbor, even when I am sick. Sometimes, my neighbor is myself, God, my family, my community, all the people and everything I encounter, and all the things I face daily. I am going to be okay. I have confidence in God, who shall call me at the hour of my death. For now, I shall remain faithful, stay calm, and be patient in dying, with the help of God.

Prayer

"My soul rests in God alone, from whom comes my salvation. God alone is my rock and salvation, my fortress; I shall never fall" (Ps 62:1–3).

O Holy Mary! My hope after Jesus, I come to you as an ungrateful child. Please pray for me, a sinner, now and at the hour of my death. Amen.

A Moment of Grace

It's important to be patient in dying. This way, you can witness the transformation from an old to a new life, a life that is a blessing. Being a Christian, "life" is life after death, and death is the end of sin, as St. Ambrose defined it. Also, patience in dying is an awesome opportunity to receive God's consolation and mercy. Do you have any fear in your life at this moment? Can you pick one or two moments from my experience and apply that to your life? You may or may not receive as I did. But keep trying, keep praying, remain faithful, and ask God for the gift of his consolation.

Finishing the Race

> Run so as to win. . . . Thus, I do not
> run aimlessly; I do not fight as if I were
> shadowboxing.
>
> —*1 Corinthians 9:24, 26*

Finishing the race is about going on living gracefully and joyfully, no matter the difficulty, until the last breath. It's also about the gift of holy perseverance.

As I write this chapter, I am still sick and receiving chemotherapy. It has been a long four years battling cancer. I must go on despite my age and fragility. So, every day, I get up and "run so as to win."

Throughout my life, there have been numerous occasions when I experienced pain. These painful experiences taught me to take courage in my suffering. Here are some examples of the four different types of pain that I endured.

Mental pain. The first time I experienced loneliness was the time I arrived at the Songkhla refugee camp in Thailand when I was eleven years old. It was my "home alone" moment. One day, I had my family; the next day, my family literally disappeared. I still remember it well. At dusk, I sat by the seashore with thousands of other refugees. There, I sat and wept and wept for missing my family. A little boy saw me weeping and asked why I was crying. I replied with more tears. It took fourteen years for my family to reappear again. Those fourteen years of loneliness helped me to be strong in facing hardship.

Physical pain. After my first year living in America, I received a major surgery to help me to walk without using crutches and braces. After the surgery, I opened my eyes: I was alone in the hospital, a newcomer to America, unable to speak English.

After eight weeks, the cast on my legs was removed, along with eighty-six stitches that had bonded together twenty-four-inch incisions on my leg and my back. At fourteen years old, this was the first physical pain that I could remember and experience. This was my "Forest Gump moment" when I could walk joyfully without crutches and braces.

Emotional pain. When I was living in Boston, I received the news that my father had lung cancer. On the day of his surgery, I came home to be with him. After visiting my parents in Charlotte, I came back to Boston. It was 10 p.m., a dark, cold, and snowy night. As I got out of the car I fell on the ground, covered with thick snow. I didn't get up and just knelt there and wept and wept.

Spiritual pain. When I discovered that I had terminal cancer I felt completely powerless and sad, and I was filled with anxiety thinking that I was going to die soon.

With each of these painful encounters, I learned to develop a "warrior mentality" toward life. One of the gifts of suffering is the ability to build character. Certainly, I obtained much wisdom through each of those moments.

Now, I have learned to bear injuries patiently and to courageously overcome any situation because I know the power of fortitude, resilience, endurance, and many other great virtues. I say these things not boastfully but with a hopeful and humble spirit. Besides, my suffering is something that I could not brag about. Rather, I want to point out the mercy of God.

In times of sickness and pain, God's mercy can be found only through God's grace. Grace alone is sufficient (see 2 Corinthians 12:9), and nothing is lacking because grace overshadows everything; "everything is grace," as St. Thérèse of Lisieux shows us in her teaching. Thus, take the courage to persevere and ask the Holy Spirit for God's grace in suffering, and let us be patient in our petition as we remain faithful to our Christian life.

Prayer

My Lord and my God, tell my soul to trust in you so that I have nothing to fear. When my season changes, from health to sickness, please plant a seed of hope so that I won't fall into despair. When loneliness comes to my door, please, Lord, let there be light, so I won't get discouraged. When the journey is hard, Lord, teach me to turn my thoughts to you—turning to you so that I can give all my troubles into your hands. Accept them, O Lord, and turn them from mourning into dancing. Then, I shall be the Lord of the dance and shall dance in the street, singing and praising your name forever and ever. Amen!

A Moment of Grace

Loneliness is part of living in this "valley of tears." It's difficult and painful. In this valley, there are many other challenges that everyone must face one way or another.

St. Alphonsus Liguori said, "In this valley of tears every man is born to weep, and all must suffer, by enduring the evils which are of daily occurrence."[1]

As Christians, each of us has the treasure and power of grace hidden within us ever since our baptism. This gift of grace shall help us overcome difficulty, hardship, trial, and tribulation. Surely, we cannot do anything without Christ. So, in a time of distress, pain, suffering, hopeless, weariness, anxiety, discouragement, fear, sickness, resentment, anguish, dying, and so on, can you put on the "armor of God" so that you may be able to stand firm (Eph 6:11) and run to win the race and not give in to despair?

A Miniature of Heaven

> What is impossible for human beings is possible for God.
>
> —*Luke 18:27*

It was the summer of 2022. I was sure my body could no longer hold my soul. The bell of death was ringing louder by the day. But as I turned my thoughts to the Lord, I received a strange invitation: "Meet me in Switzerland." And when I responded to that invitation, I experienced a miniature of heaven.

June 2022 was the most difficult month of my life. I was on palliative care because my cancer marker had jumped to the highest level since I had been diagnosed. This high number was very bad news. It seemed I was slowly dying again. I was so sick that I couldn't join my family for our summer vacation. I insisted that they go without me. They went to Norway while I stayed at home alone.

Alone at home, I was sick, weak, and armed with a bucket to catch any internal substances when vomiting struck. I looked up at the image of Jesus, and my eyes filled with tears of sorrow. Strangely, I asked the Lord for a mission impossible. I wanted to be with my family. On that day, when "I cried out, you answered" (Ps 138). Little did I know how God's mercy would rain down on my dying body.

That "mission impossible" was going to Switzerland, which had been something on my bucket list. Plus, I love the mountains, and my family planned to be there soon. After many prayers and seeking spiritual direction, I was on a two-week drug-free holiday with no treatments whatsoever. With that, I traveled alone to Switzerland in mid-July.

I arrived in Zurich a full day earlier than expected. I let my adventurous spirit lead the way. Everything was unplanned: where to sleep, eat, and go; I didn't care. I was in Switzerland, a miniature of heaven on earth. And I was happy to get lost in this Swiss paradise.

I had asked for God's mercy to do this mission impossible. Now, I had the encouragement to act so that God's mercy could reveal a miraculous phenomenon. The Lord granted me (1) the peace that I lost, (2) the strength that I didn't have, and (3) the health that I lacked.

I left my footprints on the highest mountain in Europe: climbing, hiking, walking on land, train, bus, car, and plane, gondola after gondola, ice, snow, and glacier. I had so much fun that I totally forgot about my sickness.

Nearly a week later, it was time for my family to join me in Switzerland. They were visiting our family in Norway two weeks before this occasion, without me. I returned to the airport in Zurich to pick them up. Standing outside, blending in with the natives, I was welcoming my family to Switzerland as though it were my home, my land, my country. I was back to being the father, the

A Miniature of Heaven

husband, and the man I used to be. I was back to being myself, alive again, leading, guiding, playing, and exploring the adventure of a lifetime.

We spent nearly two weeks together in Switzerland. The whole time I could not help but ponder the mystery of what had happened. Two days before the trip, I called my wife to cancel because I was so weak. But the Holy Spirit planted a seed of fortitude in me so that I could change my mind and march forward—the mission impossible.

The trip to Switzerland, alone and with family, was the perfect medicine for me. I am grateful for God's mercy. Through this mission, I learned that when I am ready to die, then I am living to the fullest.

Prayer

The Lord, my God, has clothed me in a garment of grace. Grace is with me, and nothing can harm me. My Lord suffered a great deal so that I could obtain his grace. He suffered, not so that I may not suffer, but that I may suffer just like him. For it is in suffering that the power of grace shines brightly. I shall suffer but stand firm, endure, and place my confidence in the Lord. I must be strong for the sake of my Lord and his Holy Cross.

I shall keep the faith knowing the victory prize is waiting for me. I shall march onward to the finish line and not let my heart be troubled by a little pain. I shall put on the garment of grace, and nothing shall be lacking. The Lord is my strength.

I must take courage, remain steadfast, and be faithful until the day I die. I shall never give in to despair, never. So, help me, God.

A Moment of Grace

God's superabundant strength will help us to do whatever he needs us to do. Do you need to receive God's grace? Be bold, take a risk, endure, and be patient. Without God's help, we can do nothing—but by the power of God, we can do anything.

The power of God is simple. He loves us so much that he will do anything good for us. We must trust him and be confident in his providential care. With this understanding, we can ask God for help while giving him something so that he can make what is impossible possible for us. Giving God something to work with is like the story of the boy who gave Jesus the five loaves and the two fishes that fed the five thousand men (Lk 9:16). With just some bread, fish, and courage, Jesus did an impossible thing: feeding thousands of people.

What is your "mission impossible"? Do you have something you want Jesus to know? Maybe you want to ask him for something? If so, give him something that represents a sincere and genuine gift from the bottom of your heart. Ask God to help you, and be very patient in your asking.

Part Five
The Gift of Consolation

> In going to the Shrine of Our Lady of La Vang, so dear to the hearts of the Vietnamese faithful, pilgrims entrust to her their joys and their sorrows, their hopes and their sufferings. In this way they turn to God and make themselves intercessors for their families and for their entire people . . . in order to build a world in which it is pleasant to live, based on the essential spiritual and moral values and where each person can be recognized in his dignity as a child of God, and turn freely and with filial love to his Father in heaven who is "rich in mercy" (Eph 2:4).[1]
>
> —*St. John Paul II*

For reasons known only to him, God does not always take away our suffering. And yet Our Lady stands with us, as she has always stood with me—my mother, Our Lady of Lavang, the consoler.

In this last part of the book, I am offering to you a special novena—a nine-day prayer that you can offer for any special intention, particularly when you need to experience the consolation of the Blessed Mother and her son,

Jesus. Whether you are a patient, a caregiver, or are simply experiencing some kind of unrelenting suffering of the soul, you can come to her.

Before we begin the novena, however, let me tell you a little bit about the history of the Church in Vietnam and of the way the Blessed Mother came to her poor, faithful children during one of the worst times of persecution. To them, she will always be Our Lady of Lavang, the Mother of the Suffering and Mother of Vietnam.

History of Our Lady of Lavang

> I (Mother) accepted your request. From now
> on, whoever comes to invoke me in this place,
> I will accept and bless them.
>
> —*Our Lady of Lavang, August 1798*

When we speak of redemptive suffering, we have only to look to the Blessed Mother to see the graces that are given to those who come alongside the Lord, mingling their suffering with his own. Throughout history, the Blessed Mother has appeared again and again to the poorest and neediest of her children, consoling them and comforting them. One beautiful example of this is Our Lady of Lavang, the patroness of Vietnam.

When in August 1798 King Canh Thinh banned religious instruction and ordered the destruction of churches, seminaries, and religious houses, it set off a chain of persecutions lasting more than a hundred years, with more than one hundred thousand Catholic Vietnamese martyred.

From the very beginning of the persecutions, however, the faithful continued to gather to say the Rosary. During one of these gatherings, a beautiful Lady appeared.

The Lady was in simple dress but wore a gold crown. The beautiful Lady spoke to the people as a mother, giving them words of love and comfort. She did not issue any warnings as Our Lady of Fatima did; she simply expressed her love for them as her persecuted children. Helping them with their problems and cares, she showed them how to make medicines from the plants and herbs that grew in the area. She appeared several more times, issuing the same message of love and comfort.[1]

The Lavang Church was completed in her honor over the course of fifteen years, dedicated in 1901, and destroyed by war in 1972.[2] Although the apparition is not yet officially recognized by the Vatican, her importance to the people of Vietnam was recognized by Pope John Paul II on June 19, 1998—he expressed a desire to rebuild the basilica for the two hundredth anniversary of the first vision.[3]

Novena to Our Lady of Lavang

In the name of the Father, and of the Son, and of the Holy Spirit.

O God, come to my assistance.

O Lord, make haste to help me.

Glory be to the Father . . .

Most loveable and gracious, Our Lady of Lavang, that never was it known that anyone who comes to you goes away empty-handed. Pray for me today that I always find joy in deep union with your son.

Dearest Mother, please pray for me and for these my intentions.

(State your intentions for each of the nine days, or offer each day's intention as follows.)

Day 1: By the intercession of Our Lady of Lavang, may the Lord make us worthy to see the beauty of our crosses as we follow the footsteps of our Lord Jesus Christ.

Day 2: By the intercession of Our Lady of Lavang, may the Lord make us worthy to receive grace and choose joy in suffering.

Day 3: By the intercession of Our Lady of Lavang, may the Lord make us worthy to experience God's love in times of sickness. May the Lord make us worthy to be sick for the Lord, and to die for the Lord.

Day 4: By the intercession of Our Lady of Lavang, may the Lord make us worthy to have the compassion of Jesus for others who are in pain and in need of consolation.

Day 5: By the intercession of Our Lady of Lavang, may the Lord make us worthy to love God and our neighbor as ourselves, even in times of suffering.

Day 6: By the intercession of Our Lady of Lavang, may the Lord make us worthy and deliver us from all evils and temptations as we surrender our will to God.

Day 7: By the intercession of Our Lady of Lavang, may the Lord make us worthy to forgive others as the Lord forgives us. And may the Lord make us worthy to be a source of blessing to others.

Day 8: By the intercession of Our Lady of Lavang, may the Lord make us worthy to enter the kingdom of God, both here on earth and as it is in heaven.

Day 9: By the intercession of Our Lady of Lavang, may the Lord make us worthy to win the race of life and receive the crown of victory that is waiting for us in heaven.

Hail Mary, full of grace, the Lord is with thee. Blessed art thou among women, and blessed is the fruit of thy womb, Jesus. Holy Mary, Mother of God, pray for us sinners now and at the hour of our death.

(Repeat three times.)

In the name of the Father, and of the Son, and of the Holy Spirit.
Amen.

Conclusion

I hope and pray that my life of grace will inspire you to recognize and share your own story of grace. Take courage and remain faithful to the living God in your time of trials and tribulations. Stay with Jesus as he stays with you. He is the vine, and you are his branches. In Jesus, you will bear much fruit, and everything will be all right.

May God's amazing grace be with you today and all the days of your life. May Our Lady take you by the hand and lead you closer to her beloved Son. May you always be at peace. Amen!

Notes

Part Two: The School of Suffering

Why Be "Sick for the Lord"?

    1. Attributed to Francis de Sales.

    2. Prayer before Mass attributed to Thomas Aquinas.

Suffering as Penance

    1. Attributed to Bernadette Soubirous.

    2. Attributed to Bernadette Soubirous.

    3. Attributed to Padre Pio.

    4. Antoine Marie, "Carta, January 31, 1999," Abadia de Sant Josep de Clairval, accessed March 2, 2023, https://www.clairval.com/index.php/ca/carta-ca/?id=63.

    5. Attributed to Catherine of Siena.

    6. Attributed to Arnold Janssen.

The Nails of Our Cross

    1. Attributed to Teresa of Avila.

Choose Joy

    1. Thérèse of Lisieux, *The Story of a Soul: The Autobiography of St. Thérèse of Lisieux*, trans. Thomas N. Taylor (Urbana, IL: Project Gutenberg, 2005), accessed March 3, 2023, https://www.gutenberg.org/cache/epub/16772.

Notes

Silence Is Golden

1. I adapted this prayer to my current situation. You may find the original prayer in Anselm, *Proslogion: With the Replies of Gaunilo and Anselm*, trans. Thomas Williams (Indianapolis: Hackett, 2001), 24–25.

2. Adapted from St. Patrick's Breastplate.

Grace in Suffering

1. Faustina Kowalska, *Diary of Saint Maria Faustina Kowalska: Divine Mercy in My Soul* (Stockbridge, MA: Marian Press, 2005), entry 20.

2. Attributed to Catherine of Siena.

The Ecstasy of God's Love

1. Antonio Royo Marin, *The Theology of Christian Perfection*, trans. Jordan Aumann (Eugene, OR: Wipf and Stock, 2011), 547.

When Temptation Comes

1. Attributed to Henry Suso.

Part Three: The Gift of Suffering

Tears of Love

1. Attributed to Thomas Aquinas.

Act of Surrender

1. Dolindo Ruotolo, "The Surrender Novena," Fr. Dolindo Ruotolo website, accessed February 28, 2023, https://www.fatherdolindoruotolo.com/.

Facing Reality

1. The Memorare.

Battle Fatigue

1. Régine Pernoud, *Joan of Arc: By Herself and Her Witnesses*, trans. Edward Hyams (Lanham, MD: Scarborough House, 1994), 114.

When God Speaks Forgiveness

1. From the Novena to the Immaculate Heart of Mary.

Go to Our Lady of Sorrows

1. Thomas Aquinas, *Summa Theologiae*, trans. Fathers of the English Dominican Province, I–II.38.4.

Part Four: The Way to New Life

1. Bernadatte Soubirous, quoted in Marie Aloysia Dunne, "The Homecoming of the Lamb," *The Rosary Magazine* vol. 33, July–December 1908, 676.

The End of the Road

1. Ambrose of Milan, quoted in Willian Theodore Wiesner, "De Bono Mortis: A Revised Text with an Introduction, Translation, and Commentary" (PhD diss., The Catholic University of America, 1970), 105.

2. English translation of the "Canticle of Simeon" by the International Commission on English Texts.

Finishing the Race

1. Alphonsus Liguori, *The Glories of Mary*, ed. Robert Coffin (London: Burns and Oates, 1868), 420.

Part Five: The Gift of Consolation

1. Message of John Paul II for the Conclusion of the Marian Year in La Vang, Vietnam, July 16, 1999, no. 3, https://www.vatican.va/content/john-paul-ii/en/letters/1999/documents/hf_jp-ii_let_19990716_madonna-la-vang.html.

History of Our Lady of Lavang

1. Eleonore Villarrubia, "Our Lady of La Vang: The Catholic Side of Vietnam," Catholicism.org, January 24, 2013, https://catholicism.org/our-lady-of-la-vang-the-catholic-side-of-vietnam.html.

2. Luna Nguyen, "The Story of Our Lady of Lavang," *Catholic Pilgrimage Network*, April 12, 2018, https://catholicpilgrimagenetwork.com/the-story-of-our-lady-of-lavang/.

3. Since the American involvement in the Vietnam War of the 1960s and 1970s, and the loss of that war, many Vietnamese fled their homeland and settled in other parts of the world, taking their faith and their Virgin with them. I have found at least five parishes in the United States named for their national patroness. They are located in far-flung parts of our country—Houston, Texas; Santa Ana, California; Portland, Oregon; Baltimore, Maryland; and New Orleans, Louisiana.

Peter Le is a Vietnamese Catholic who is executive director and founder—with his wife, Dr. ThuHuong Trinh—of St. Joseph Primary Care, a nonprofit medical clinic that provides health care services in line with Church teaching.

Born during the Vietnam War, Le came to the United States as a thirteen-year-old polio survivor among the "boat people" of the 1980s. Diagnosed with thyroid cancer in 2018, Le has dedicated his life to sharing his story with those overwhelmed by suffering and hardship.

Le earned a bachelor's degree in computer engineering from the University of Houston in 1995. He previously worked as a software developer and IT analyst for Duke Cancer Institute and as a medical education specialist for Harvard Medical School.

Le lives with his family in Raleigh, North Carolina.

www.tobesick.com

Facebook: https://www.facebook.com/peterhuyle.nc